A FUNNY THING HAPPENED ON THE WAY TO DEMENTIA

A Stand Up Comedian's Race Against Time

By Sharon Lacey

MOtivational
LEADERS IN GLOBAL PUBLISHING

Published by Motivational Press, Inc.
1777 Aurora Road
Melbourne, Florida, 32935
www.MotivationalPress.com

Manufactured in the United States of America.

ISBN: 978-1-62865-370-0

CONTENTS

ACKNOWLEDGMENTS **8**

PROLOGUE **9**

PART ONE

CHAPTER 1
DEMENTIA **11**

CHAPTER 2
A NEW BEGINNING **15**

CHAPTER 3
LEARNING THE CRAFT **20**

CHAPTER 4
TUITION **24**

CHAPTER 5
DEDICATION, INSPIRATION, HUMILIATION **31**

CHAPTER 6
MY FIRST BIG SHOW **37**

CHAPTER 7
WHO AM I? **40**

CHAPTER 8
ROAD COMIC **42**

CHAPTER 9
IRAQ **56**

CHAPTER 10
CRAZY GIGS **72**

CHAPTER 11
ONE DOOR CLOSES AS ANOTHER DOOR OPENS **74**

CHAPTER 12
SHE SLEEPS IN HER CAR??! **76**

CHAPTER 13
BACK TO IRAQ **80**

CHAPTER 14
UGANDAN SOLDIERS **85**

PART TWO

CHAPTER 15
OFF TO AFRICA. **88**

CHAPTER 16
THE LONG JOURNEY **90**

CHAPTER 17
NILE AND SAFARI! **93**

CHAPTER 18
BACK TO THE PEARL **106**

CHAPTER 19
TANDEM HOTEL **108**

CHAPTER 20
TRAGEDY AND COMEDY **113**

CHAPTER 21
SCHOOL IN BBIRA **116**

CHAPTER 22
WHAT I LIKE ABOUT U...GANDA **128**

CHAPTER 23
THE ELDERS. **135**

CHAPTER 24
THE BARBER **138**

CHAPTER 25
CHRISTMAS IN AFRICA **141**

CHAPTER 26
FUN GONE WRONG **148**

CHAPTER 27
WILD GORILLAS. **151**

CHAPTER 28
SAYING GOODBYE **173**

CHAPTER 29
A FUNNY THING HAPPENED... . . . . **175**

Cover Photo: A field of giant white concrete ears of corn in Ohio. Sharon couldn't resist taking a photo while standing behind one.

To my maternal grandmother, my mom, and my daughter.

The timeline of some of the events in this book have been altered for continuity and brevity.

ACKNOWLEDGMENTS

I'd like to thank my daughter, Shawna, and my friends, Megan Davidson and Jessica Richman, for generously giving their time in proofreading this book. Their suggestions were invaluable, and their contributions to this labor of love will forever be remembered and appreciated.

PROLOGUE

"And the winner of the 1965 Washington State Fair Talent Contest is Sharon Galloway!"

I was ten years old. Applause carried me up to the stage where I excitedly collected the First Place trophy for the comedic monologue I had performed in front of hundreds of fairgoers. *Thrilling* didn't even begin to describe the feeling!

The next day I was stripped of my title. The rules stated that all contestants must be at least twelve years old. After her parents objected to my win, the fourteen-year old second-place winner was given my trophy.

Of course it hurt, but I knew who had really won. What I didn't know was that forty years later I would get back on stage and continue my career as a stand up comedian.

PART ONE

CHAPTER 1

DEMENTIA

"Grama. We're all here with you. We love you. Let go if you want to."

Now forty-five years old, married and with a daughter, I was standing next to my dying grandmother's bed in the Alzheimer's Unit. It might have been a dumb thing to say. So cliché. Melodramatic. But as I stood there holding my grandmother's hand, it seemed like the right thing to say. A few minutes later, she exhaled for the final time.

Grama was an amazing woman. She held a job outside the home long before it was the norm. She was an excellent cook, a master knitter, and kept a neat and tidy home. She enjoyed camping, hiking, and walked two miles a day, even in her eighties.

I loved how she'd say, "Oh scaaattie!" if we sneezed when we were little, or how she'd shake her head and say, "Ohhhh Lorrrd...." when something went wrong. What I loved most about her, though, was that she never said an unkind word to or about anyone. I could talk to her and share my innermost feelings, and she would listen attentively and with compassion. I felt closer to her than anyone else in the world.

One afternoon, when Grama was about eighty-five years old, we went for a walk in her neighborhood. She lived alone in a nice mobile home park for senior citizens. My parents, sister, and I had all noticed that for the past several months Grama had been asking us questions within a few minutes of having already asked us or repeating something that she had said just minutes before. We were all worried about her, but didn't want to let her know what we all had been suspecting for some time.

"Honey, I'm thinking maybe I should move to a care center." She sounded worried, and a little scared at the same time.

"Why, Grama?"

"Well...I think maybe I'm starting to get that Alzheimer's disease we heard about on the news the other night. Things just don't seem right anymore."

Not long after that, we settled her into a senior care center. That insidious mind-robbing disease took her away, little by little. As time went by, she was unable to hold a conversation. No longer did she seem to be cognizant of where she was or who we were. She was moved to the Alzheimer's Unit. It was heartbreaking to see such a vital, caring person go through this slow decline. I didn't want to let her go. One afternoon I was showing her the family photo album, hoping that something might jog her memory. It was clear that she didn't recognize any of us, and I was overcome with profound sadness. I looked her in the eyes and said deeply from my heart, "I love you Grama."

She looked at me in surprise, and said, "Well, I love you, too, Sharon!" She was there! She was right there with me and knew who I was! A moment later she was gone again, back in the dementia prison. Those precious few seconds of clarity were the last I would have with her. She died at age ninety-one.

Five years later, my mom began showing signs of the disease as well. She was just seventy-two. *No! Not Mom, too. Not so soon.*

This isn't supposed to happen. All of the magazine articles and news reports about Alzheimer's had said that exercise, eating right, and keeping your brain active would keep the disease at bay. My mom, even in her sixties, still played softball, worked at the high school, and ran her own ceramics business in the basement. Now she was into making intricate quilts and loving retirement. She was NOT supposed to get Alzheimer's! Having seen her own mother slowly lose her mind and life to the disease, I know my mom was scared.

Mom and Grama loved being active year round

Now I was scared, too. Was I next? At this accelerating rate, would I have Alzheimer's by the time I turned sixty? I began noticing lapses in my own memory. Friends assured me it was just normal aging; that I was worrying over nothing. As a middle school teacher, I prided myself on remembering the names of my students – from *all twenty-one years* of teaching. It was getting more difficult to remember names, recall facts, to find the right word. And I was only fifty.

I figured it was just a matter of time before Alzheimer's took over my life too. *If that's the case,* I told myself, *I'd better make the most of the time my brain has left. If Alzheimer's is going to strike me, I'll at least go down fighting every step of the way.*

A funny thing happened on the way to dementia: My journey as a standup comedian began.

CHAPTER 2

A NEW BEGINNING

"Coming up to the stage now is a newbie. She's never been to an open mic before, so please take it easy on her. Let's have a big round of applause for Sharon Lacey!"

My job as a middle school teacher was challenging, but I loved it. I had even won national recognition and awards for my creative teaching methods. The articles about fending off Alzheimer's disease all stated that we must continue making new connections in our brains, with doing crossword puzzles or Sudoku the routinely suggested solution. That just sounded boring to me. *Maybe I should try doing stand up comedy*, I thought. I loved being on stage getting laughs when I was a kid. Why not try it again? Not as a career, of course, just as a fun hobby. A way to make my brain work a little harder, and a way to get out of the house to meet new people, now that our daughter had grown up and moved away. Of course, being a kid and reciting a monologue someone else wrote is a lot easier than writing and performing your own material. What did I really know about stand up comedy? I'd never even been to a live comedy show.

Someone told me that comedians start out by going to open mics, where they perform about three minutes of material. So now, at age fifty, I decided to give it a try.

Comedy open mics are generally held in bars. I never went to bars. A few years earlier, my college-aged daughter and her roommate had invited me to go to a tavern to see one of their favorite bands. I was thrilled that they had asked me to go with them, but I was also nervous. What would I wear? I didn't want to look like a frumpy mom. And what would I drink? I hated the taste of beer and wine and I had no clue what kind of mixed drink to order. When we went into the tavern, I was obviously the oldest person in the place. I was so nervous that when the waitress asked me what I wanted to drink, I just said the first thing that came to mind. "A shot of tequila?"

"Wow, Sharon!" my daughter's roommate said admiringly. "You're bad ass!"

I promptly lost all "bad ass" credibility as I took tiny sips of the tequila and made it last for two hours.

The girls wanted me to dance with them. "No way!" I exclaimed and shrank even farther back into the booth where we were sitting. I couldn't dance. I'd never had a boyfriend, or a husband for that matter, who had been willing to get out on the dance floor with me, so I just never learned. It would be way too embarrassing to go into that crowd of people and try to dance.

"Well then," my daughter said, "we'll just have to dance right here, sitting down!" They proceeded to wiggle around on the bench and clap their hands in the air and on the table to the beat of the music. Now *that* I could do. It ended up being a super fun night.

But now, three years later, I was going to a bar again and might even get up on stage and perform. I didn't want to go alone. I asked my husband, Clint, to go with me. I wasn't surprised when he said he didn't want to. Convincing Clint to go anywhere with me had always been a monumental task. We'd been married twenty-six years and he liked his routine of going to work, coming home, and nestling into his La-Z-Boy for the remainder of the evening. He didn't want to go to some tavern.

"Come on, pleeeeeeeze?" I pleaded. "We don't have to stay long."

I begged and cajoled, and finally wore him down. An hour later, we were sitting in the small audience at a place that had a weekly comedy night.

As we sat in that smoky lounge, I was surprised that all of the "comedians" who went up on stage were young guys in their early twenties. They each did about three minutes' time. Most of their material was extremely raunchy. *I think I can do this. I know the F-word!* I decided to go put my name on the sign-up sheet. But as I tried to get up, Clint grabbed my arm and yanked me back down.

"No! Don't do this! You'll make a fool of yourself. Wait until some other time," my husband warned.

He was trying to save me from certain humiliation. I'm not one to turn down a challenge though. It quickly became apparent I'm not one to shy away from embarrassing situations either. I pulled away and rushed over to the emcee.

"Is it too late to sign up?" I asked.

"Hell, no!" he grinned. "Here's a pen. Go for it!" I wrote my name on the sign-up sheet. I was #8 on the list.

By the time I got back to my seat, #5 was up. My mind was racing. Would I be able to remember the two minutes of material I'd written a week earlier? Would I get any laughs? My hands began to shake.

When #6 went up, my legs also began to shake. What had I done? I took a few deep breaths. *Calm down, Sharon,* I chided myself. It didn't help.

Now #7 was up. I tried to reassure myself. *Think about your first line, Sharon. Just remember those first few words and the rest will follow.* But now even my boobs were shaking. My boobs? How does that even happen? Maybe there was still time to go back over there and cross out my name.

But before I could do that, my name was called. Every inch of my body was now shaking. *Why am I so nervous? I get up in front of middle school students every day, don't I? True...but they rely on me for a grade – they HAVE to laugh at my jokes. These adults don't!*

Trying not to trip, I mounted the few steps to the stage and crossed over to the center. The spotlight was blinding; I couldn't see anyone in the audience. I figured I'd better go a little raunchy like the young guys had done, since that seemed to be what the audience wanted. So I took a deep breath, stepped up to the microphone, and said, "Um...my boobs are shaking."

The audience roared with laughter!

"So...my husband asked me out on a date last week. We never go on dates! It was the middle of the afternoon. He wouldn't tell me where we were going. I thought maybe we were heading to a matinee...maybe a walk in the park. I asked for a hint. He said he was getting some professional pictures taken. How romantic! But it turned out he was going to get his first colonoscopy."

I thought I heard a couple polite chuckles.

"Apparently he wanted me to come along for moral support. Yeah, (sarcastically) that's my idea of a fun date. Watching my man get Roto-Rootered."

I heard a few more chuckles. I kept going. "No, really, that's my idea of a fun date!"

More laughs.

"So there he was, half naked on the exam table, just looking so pitiful. I thought maybe I should light a few candles...put on some Barry White."

That got a good laugh.

"But then the doctor came in, and one thought entered my head: *Threesome!*"

The laughs were loud now. This was fun!

"I figured I should give my man some encouragement. 'Hey there, Cupcake... Remember that little back door play you're so fond of asking for? Your turn!'"

Raucous laughter filled the place. I gave a quick bow and hurried back to my seat. I hoped Clint would be waiting for me with a big high-five or maybe a pat on the back. Nope. He was slumped down in his seat, looking down at his hands with embarrassment. Whether it was about my performance or that he was the butt of the joke, I wasn't sure. Either way, I figured I wouldn't be asking him to come along with me the next time. As it turned out, there were a lot of "next times."

CHAPTER 3

LEARNING THE CRAFT

For the next three months, I went to every open mic I could find. The comedy bug had bitten me, and I wanted to learn as much as I could. If someone would give me stage time within a four-hour drive from Portland, I'd go there to perform for three to seven minutes. I often made the journey up I-5 to Seattle to do the open mic at the Seattle Comedy Underground on Monday evenings. Carl, the club manager, would give me an extra minute of stage time because he knew I'd driven four hours to get there. I really appreciated that. Then I'd hurry back down to Portland the same night so I could teach school the next day. I definitely was pushing my brain to work harder!

Hanging out in the comedy clubs and open mic bars, I was immersed in a completely foreign culture. More often than not, the majority of the people in the audience at the open mics were other comedians waiting for stage time. As a teacher, I always required my students to be kind and supportive to each other. No bullying allowed. If someone gave a book report or presentation in front of the class, the students were all required to listen politely and applaud at the end. Those guidelines seemed to be unheard of at the open mics. I was surprised at first to find that lots of the other comics would sit or stand in the back of the room, half-listening or talking through the other comics' sets. It seemed like the only way to get the comics to laugh at your jokes was to be as raunchy as possible.

Luckily, I was smart enough to keep my opinions to myself, and the young comics accepted me into their group. Apparently I looked younger than my age because most of them assumed I was in my late thirties or early forties. When I overheard them mocking some of the older, fifty-something established comics, I was afraid I'd be their next target. So I kept my mouth shut about my age. They didn't need to know that I had a daughter their age.

There were very few women in the open mic scene back then, and like most of the guys, they were all in their twenties or early thirties. Everyone was easygoing, street smart, and edgy. They all got a kick out of teasing me for being an innocent, naive middle school teacher. And it was true - I was definitely naïve about the ways of their world. I'd spent the previous thirty years putting myself through college, getting married, having a career in radio and television, then a career as a teacher, and raising a daughter. I didn't spend my hard-earned dollars on cheap beer (PBR was their beer of choice. I had no idea that 'PBR' stood for 'Pabst Blue Ribbon'), cigarettes, or drugs. I certainly didn't have all night to hang out in bars. I'd always arrive early so I could be near the top of the lineup, then hurry home after my set to finish grading papers and write lesson plans. Before I could start on my homework, though, I first needed to take a shower and wash the clothes I'd been wearing to get rid of the cigarette smoke that permeated my hair and clothing.

The guys took me under their wing, giving me tips to better my stage presence. "Don't look down so much!" "Let go of the mic cord; it makes you look nervous." "Don't sit on the stool. Only lazy comics do that." "Don't end with 'that's my time' – you can come up with something better than that." "Make sure you never go over your allotted time. If you're given three minutes, get off that stage in three minutes." I tried to soak up every piece of advice. I watched the other comics, tried to learn from what they did right, and what they didn't do well.

There were plenty of times when I'd be on stage at the open mics and bomb. We all did. At first, it felt awful to bomb. But then one of the more experienced comics, Lonnie Bruhn, took me aside and gave me some valuable advice. He told me to bomb on purpose the next time I go on stage. He said that if I would bomb on purpose, I'd see that it's survivable. It would force me to find ways to get out of the hole, so to speak. He also told me when I was hanging my head after a particularly bad set that rather than moping around feeling embarrassed or humiliated, I should be spending my time trying to learn from that set. I needed to study it and figure out what I could do differently the next time.

Someone else pointed out that stand up comedy is the one career where you must fail repeatedly in front of a crowd in order to improve. You can be absolutely, undeniably, totally hilarious at home in front of your bedroom mirror. Until you stand up in front of a crowd and try that joke however, you won't really know if it's going to work. Knowing that it was okay – even *expected* – to bomb, helped remove some of the pressure.

I also went to a comedy class offered at the local community college. A local comedy booker was the guest speaker. He told us to write down what we thought the most important factor is in being a successful stand up comedian. Most of us wrote down "be funny".

"If you wrote the words 'be funny', you would be wrong," he said. "Comedy is show business. And if the BUSINESS doesn't come first, you won't have a show. You can be the funniest person in the world, but if you don't know how to find the work and handle the business, you're going to go nowhere."

His words were a huge relief to me because, honestly, I wasn't all that funny. Some people have this natural comedic talent and everything that comes out of their mouth is hilarious. I'm not one of those people. I have to work really hard to write jokes. It doesn't come easy to me. Ever. The only thing that did come easy to me was looking for gigs, calling bookers and club owners, and following through.

At first, I pretty much did what most novice comedians do: I took the easy way out and wrote raunchy material. It's not hard to get laughs simply by shocking the audience. After spending twenty-one politically correct years as a teacher who never used foul language or even had bad thoughts, it felt liberating to go to the other end of the spectrum for a change. So if going "blue" would get the open mic audience and other comics to laugh and listen, that is what I would do. I always felt conflicted about it though. It just wasn't the "real me." It would take a few more years before I could finally be ME on stage.

Somewhere along the way, I began to forget about doing stand up as just a hobby. I liked the challenge of trying to get paid bookings and it certainly was making my brain step it up in the memory department. Now the question was: How would I get that first booking? And how would I do in front of a real, paying audience?

CHAPTER 4
TUITION

Those questions were answered when I got my first "big break". Headliner Cain Lopez and feature act Roger Lizaola needed a ride to a bar show in Oak Harbor, about nine hours from Portland. If I gave them a ride, they'd let me emcee their show. The emcee is the person who starts the show, doing a ten to fifteen minute set, then introduces the next two acts. The feature act comes next, with a twenty to thirty minute set, and the headliner finishes the show with a forty-five to sixty minute set.

That was my first paid gig. Actually, Cain slipped me $50 under the table to help pay for gas, but I called it a paid gig. I was clearly a novice: I have no doubt that I was an absolutely terrible emcee. In fact, anyone who has been in this business for long knows that emceeing is one of the most challenging jobs in comedy.

There were about forty people in the audience. They were loud and excited as they waited for the show to begin. They'd obviously already had a lot to drink, so I hoped that maybe they'd be too drunk to notice how inexperienced I was.

"Don't worry, kid," Cain encouraged me, even though he was half my age. "You're gonna do just fine."

I wasn't so sure about that, as I stepped onto the stage and tried not to squint into the spotlight.

"How's everyone doing?" I started out. I'd yet to learn that this is a tired, hacky way of starting a show.

The audience gave the requisite hoots and hollers in reply.

"I'm a middle school teacher," I said, taking the microphone out of its stand. "But I like doing stand up comedy better. For one thing, there aren't as many pregnant girls here."

Lots of bawdy laughter. "The hardest thing about teaching middle school is trying to find time to go to the bathroom. I just think hearing your teacher pee is a little too much information."

No laughs on that. I kept going. "So I have to go when the girls are supposed to be in class. Only I have to hurry, or those girls will come in who've conned their male teachers into letting them out of class early. You know, the period fakers?"

That got some laughs. "We female teachers don't fall for that crap. 'Really, AGAIN this week?' "

Lots more laughter. I sat on the stool in the middle of the stage. "So I finally get into my little stall (*I looked at the imaginary school bathroom stall wall, and slumped in defeat*) and I see they've written stuff about me."

Big laughs. I pointed to the imaginary wall, reading: "'*Miss Lacey's a bitch*'. That's Christa's handwriting."

Even more laughs. "I am so... (*I pretended to be angry or near tears, but then happily proclaimed*) ...proud of her. She remembered the *T* in *bitch!*"

I got huge laughs on that line. The rest of my set was just mediocre and I rushed the lines when the laughs didn't come.

But the audience was polite, and Cain and Roger couldn't have been nicer to me when the show was over.

After this trip, things started happening. I got my first Tribble Run just eight months after my first open mic, traveling with headliner Robin Cee to perform in bars all across Idaho and Montana. A Tribble Run is the name given to the chains of Pacific Northwest gigs booked by David Tribble. The gigs didn't pay much and involved long drives that sometimes stretched for twelve hours across Oregon, Idaho, and Montana. In fact, after paying for half the gas, I barely broke even as the feature act. But I loved every moment of every Run. For a beginning comedian, this was exactly the kind of experience I needed. If you can get laughs in a lounge bar in Idaho Falls where the audience is only there to kill time before the dancing begins, you can handle almost anything. More Tribble Runs followed, traveling with other headliners. I loved listening to their stories on those long runs and getting advice from them.

A few other bookers were willing to give me a chance too. The one who helped me the most was Andre' Paradise. I met Dre', as he liked to be called, at Harvey's Comedy Club in Portland. I had gone there for the usual Sunday night open mic. But instead of an open mic, they were having auditions for some big opportunity. I was so green/naïve/stupid/brazen that I decided to throw my name in the hat too. I'm quite sure I was the worst one who auditioned! Dre' must have liked my willingness to put myself out there though, because he offered to include me in some shows he booked. If I was willing to put in the effort and drive to towns and cities an hour or two from my Portland home, he was willing to give me stage time. So I did! I'd drive forty-five minutes every week to get five minutes of stage time in front of a paying audience. I didn't get paid, but as I improved, Dre' gave me more stage time: seven minutes, ten minutes, fifteen minutes. Other open mic comics scoffed at me for driving so far to do those gigs without pay. For me, it wasn't about getting paid. It was about getting better, about learning the craft and having the opportunity to perform in front of an actual audience, not just other beginning comedians.

Some people call this unpaid stage of a comedy career "paying your dues." Master comedian Debbie Wooten gave me a better analogy: Tuition. If you want to become a professional in many other careers, you pay big bucks to go to college and attend classes. All of those unpaid or low paid gigs were simply my tuition, and my classroom was the stage. What a wonderful, scary, fun, and terrifying way to get an education! But what a fantastic adventure!

Andre' Paradise was instrumental in helping me "learn by fire." I learned how to deal with drunk crowds, young crowds, black crowds, redneck crowds, and college crowds. To be kind, I guess you could say I did "okay." I was NOT good, that's for sure. Who is though, when they're first starting out, unless they're natural comedians, and I was definitely not a natural. For the most part, the audiences would laugh politely, probably mostly out of pity. They could tell I was a newbie. When people filed past us after the shows, they'd enthusiastically shower the headliner and feature acts with compliments, gushing about how hilarious they were. Then they'd either pass by me without comment or say, "Oh – you were funny, too," apparently wanting to spare my feelings. Eventually, as I began to improve, Dre' gave me paid spots, and also let me enter his Shades of Laughs Urban Comedy Competition. I didn't get very far in the competition, but it was another learning opportunity.

While doing all of this, I was still a full time teacher. There were occasions when I'd get up at 7am, teach school all day, race to my car as soon as school was out, fight rush hour traffic to get to my gig five hours away in a casino in Coos Bay, do two back-to-back shows, then drive back home to Portland, and get three hours of sleep before getting up to start another school day. I should've felt exhausted, but I didn't; I felt exhilarated!

I knew I couldn't keep up this pace forever though. I was a dedicated teacher; the kind who usually stayed at work long after the students and other teachers had gone home and still took work home with me. I loved my students and wanted to give them the best experience possible in my classroom. If I needed to teach about Early Man, I'd spend the weekend transforming my classroom into a cave. I'd push all of the desks together, and cover them with vines and foliage I'd bought at a craft shop. I'd cover the "cave" floor with fake furs I'd bought at thrift stores. I even found a fake log fire to put in a corner of the "cave." On Monday morning, the students would be greeted by a strange cavewoman. She'd grunt at them and motion them to crawl into the classroom – er, cave. They knew the cavewoman was their crazy teacher; they'd come to expect surprises like this from me. Inside the cave, they made paintbrushes out of sticks and crow feathers. They made paints by mashing berries and raw eggs. Then they learned about the ancient cave paintings found in Lascaux, France.

Each year my students would write a screenplay, and then we'd spend a Friday night at school shooting the movie. After all the scenes were shot, we'd have pizza. Then I'd send them on a treasure hunt in the school, following clues I had prepared for them. Next came the highlight of the evening: Hide and seek!

The three parent chaperones and I would find separate hiding places somewhere in the school, and the students would have thirty minutes to find us. Then all of the students would hide, and the chaperones and I would have thirty minutes to find them. For five years in a row, I held the record of not being found! I hid under a big box that was covered with school supplies in my own classroom. Of course, we only went into the areas where we had permission to go, and we always made sure to clean up the school and leave everything so orderly that no one could tell we'd spent the night at school.

Before switching to middle school, I had also taught 6th grade in elementary schools for many years. At the end of each school year, I'd have a Parent Night. I would surprise my students and their parents with a video I had made, showing all of the highlights of their year in my class.

Just before each class graduated from high school, several years after being in my 6th grade class, I would invite them all back to our classroom for a reunion. We'd talk and laugh about the fun times we'd had and the many things they had learned. I'd show them the movie they made, then play the highlight video from our year together. We'd take a new class picture, and I'd put it in my Memory Book alongside their previous picture from years earlier.

One year, a fellow teacher nominated me for the Disney American Teacher Award. This is much like the Academy Awards, only for teachers. I was among 8,000 teachers nominated for these national awards that year and I won in my category! My husband and I were flown to Los Angeles and given a room for a week in the Ritz Carlton, along with the other finalists, courtesy of Disney. We got free passes to Disneyland and enjoyed dinner in Walt Disney's private dining room. Best of all, the other teachers and I were on a televised awards show where the winners were announced. Before the show taping, we all were given formal gowns and tuxedos to wear, and we walked the red carpet. Famous celebrities gave us our trophies, just like at the Oscars!

Obviously, I loved my job as a teacher, but I also loved this new career as a comedian. I felt like it was really challenging my brain in new ways, helping me fend off Alzheimer's. To be a full-time comedian though, meant being on the road for weeks at a time. There was no way I could accept long road gigs during the school year. I was eight to ten years away from retirement, yet didn't want to put my comedy on hold. So I had to make a HUGE decision: Should I abandon my teaching career?

CHAPTER 5

DEDICATION, INSPIRATION, HUMILIATION

Compromise came in the form of a one year unpaid leave from teaching. During that year, I tried to make good use of the time. If I wasn't doing a paid gig, I was at an open mic. Six or seven nights a week out working on my writing, delivery, networking. Comedy was my job.

My age and frugality turned out to be an advantage. My husband and I always paid cash for our cars, our home mortgage was paid off, and our daughter was grown and living on her own. Our few bills were pretty easy to handle with only Clint's income. We had savings to fall back on if needed. Most of the young comics had to keep their day jobs to pay their rent. They couldn't just leave everything to go do low-paying feature jobs on the road for weeks at a time. A number of the young guys didn't even have cars or if they did, it might not have survived the long trips. Tribble Runs to Montana, gigs at casinos in northwestern Washington, one-nighters in southern Oregon, emceeing at Harvey's in Portland or at the Seattle Comedy Underground; if there was stage time and someone was willing to book me, I took it.

My good credit score also gave me an advantage. Credit card companies often sent me offers of free flights if I'd simply sign up for their card. Free flights meant I could venture a little farther away from home.

I spent five days in San Francisco, performing at every venue that would allow me onto their stage. It was a fun adventure, flying to Oakland and then taking the BART subway to the heart of San Francisco. I found an inexpensive place to stay and began exploring the city. I found an open mic in a laundromat called Brain Wash. The comics there were friendly and welcoming. Next I went to a tiny hole in the wall comedy venue called "Our Little Theater" that could seat about ten people. The Indian woman who ran the room, Sia Amma, gave me stage time and some sage advice:

"While much of the world believes that women are not funny, don't think of it as true. When you don't do well on stage, don't worry too much about it. Kick off your shoes, have a drink, have sex, and the next day pick up where you left off. Whatever you do, don't give up; get back into the business of telling jokes. Comedy is a process, and you must have a solid ground to stand on. That only comes by doing it over and over and over."

Sia's advice, along with that of many other people I met along the way, gave me comfort and served me well in my journey through comedy. It's very easy to doubt yourself in this line of work. You need a hard shell and thick skin if you want to be a comedian. I had neither. Whenever I came across a piece of advice that seemed to give me courage to keep going, I wrote it down and kept it in the front of a notebook:

"They said I was the fighter who got knocked down the most. I also got up the most." Floyd Patterson

"If you're going to fail, at least fail doing something you love." Johnny Carson

"Those who dare to fail miserably can achieve greatly." Robert Kennedy

"The person who goes farthest is generally the one who is willing to do and dare. The sure thing boat never gets far from shore." Dale Carnegie

"You might run into people who are much more talented than you; but make sure that no one out-works you." Derek Jeter

"The harder you work, the luckier you get." Motivational poster in my classroom

I looked at these quotes often on days when I felt like giving up.

Like I said, I wasn't a natural talent and wasn't good at writing jokes. Although I loved getting up in front of an audience, my delivery was less than spectacular. I didn't sound believable, but rather like I was faking trying to sound natural. It sounded rehearsed. Memorized. Awful. Annoying, even. I KNEW this, but didn't know how to fix it. Knowing you're not very good might be the place where you give up, but I refused.

Most headliners I worked with were tolerant of my lack of experience. I often asked for their advice and constructive criticism, and they gave me a lot of great pointers. I always wrote down their advice, and referred to it often.

One local headliner really went above and beyond what was necessary to humiliate me though. My home club, Harvey's Comedy Club, was televising a show. I was supposed to do a ten minute set at the beginning, before the cameras started rolling, to warm up the audience. However, just before I was to go on stage, the headliner suddenly decided to go up and do a few minutes first. He was hilarious, and really got the crowd going. Unfortunately, and as no surprise to me, I couldn't follow him. My set just didn't stand up to his, and I understandably got a mediocre response from the audience who had just been wowed by the headliner. That was humiliating enough. But then the headliner came back up on stage as I was walking off stage, and announced gleefully into the microphone, "EWWWWWW!!! Thaaaaaaaat was BAAAAAD!!!!!!! I mean THAAAAAAT was REAAAAAALLLLLY BAAAAAAAD!!!!!" He got everyone laughing along with him about how much my set stunk. He kept it going as I walked the long walk of shame all the way around the back perimeter of the room behind the audience, until I could slink into the back room. I won't lie; I sat there in that room and cried.

Years later, he and I talked about that night. He said he was just giving me the ol' initiation treatment. I still don't think it was necessary to do that to me, but he and I have become good friends. Even so, I have to admit I took some pleasure in hearing about what another novice comedian did to him when they were out on the road. When the headliner tried to "initiate by humiliation", the newbie comic got in the car and drove the four hours back to Portland, stranding the headliner at the gig. Karma?

Two other established headliners who've been in the business for more than twenty years have both told me they used to cringe when they'd watch me perform in those early days. Hey, I don't blame them. I videotaped most of my performances so that I could learn from my mistakes, and I cringed too. First I would pick myself apart for the way I looked. *You're too fat. Your hair looks awful. You need to wear a better outfit.* If I could get past that, I could finally focus on trying to improve my delivery and material. I knew I had a lot to learn. But so does every comedian when they start out. I wasn't going to give up.

It was a comedian named Barbara May from Edmonton, Canada, who helped me fix my terrible delivery. We were on the road together, traveling across Alberta and British Columbia, playing in small clubs along the way. We got to know each other well enough to be honest with each other. When she came right out and told me that I sounded fake on stage, I really appreciated it. I told her I agreed with her, but that I didn't know how to overcome it.

"Meet me at the club two hours early tonight," she said as she dropped me off at the hotel to get ready for that night's show.

As instructed, I showed up two hours early.

"Go on stage and say the first line of your joke," Barbara ordered from where she sat in the back row of the empty showroom.

I walked onto the stage and stepped up to the microphone. "My best friend Jackie is so mad at her boyfriend. It turns out he-"

"STOP! CUT!" Barbara interrupted me. "I don't believe you. Start over."

"Okay.... My best friend Jackie is so mad at her boyfriend-"

"NOPE! You sound fake. Do it again."

"My best friend Jackie-"

"NO! Sharon, you sound like you are simply saying lines that you've memorized. No one would believe that you really have a best friend Jackie-"

This time I interrupted her. "Well, I actually DON'T have a best friend Jackie..."

"I don't care! It doesn't matter! If you're going to say you have a best friend Jackie, then it'd better be believable. Now try again.

Only this time, forget the microphone. Just pretend like you're talking to me, not an audience."

I tried again.

"Better! Yes! Okay, keep going...." Barbara encouraged me.

An hour later I finally got the seal of approval from Barbara, and was relieved to stop sounding rehearsed. It was such a generous thing for her to do for me. In this competitive field, she could just as easily have let me flounder. Instead, she gave her own time to help me learn and lift me up. I owe a lot to her.

CHAPTER 6

MY FIRST BIG SHOW

Some people think they're ready to feature or headline as soon as they've done their first open mic. Much to the consternation of veteran comics, some newbies have the audacity to call themselves "comedians" even though they've never had a paid gig and earned the title. They're eager and excited and want to move ahead as quickly as possible. Not a good idea. Biting off more than you can chew before you're truly ready can leave you un-bookable. If a club owner or booker takes a chance on you, only to find that you really aren't as good as you sold yourself to be, they'll never book you again. Experienced comics say it takes a minimum of five years, but usually much longer, to start headlining shows.

The owner of Harvey's, Barry Kolen, made a rare exception for me. He knew I wasn't ready to headline, but allowed me to put on a show to benefit a school scholarship fund IF I could drum up an audience. I passed out fliers in neighborhoods, went to all of the area schools inviting their staffs, notified the local newspapers, and went on a local TV station's morning talk show. The room was nearly sold out! I did thirty minutes on the main stage at Harvey's, and an experienced headliner finished the show.

I had invited my husband, Clint, to attend. I thought he'd be pretty impressed with how far I had come since that very first open mic a year earlier. As I was doing my act, I'd glance at him from the stage. He never cracked a smile. Afterward, I asked him what he thought of my act. "Welllllllll," he said hesitantly, "you weren't *bad*. I mean, you weren't *BAD* bad." I was so hurt. Even if I was the worst comic he'd ever seen in his life, couldn't he have lied and said I was hilarious? Then again, did I really need or want false praise? I decided it was probably best to just stop inviting him to my shows for now.

Also in the audience that night were several of my peers from schools where I had taught, parents of some of my former students, and some school administrators. This presented a dilemma. All of them knew me as a squeaky clean, politically correct, award-winning teacher. My material didn't reflect that. Instead, it presented a former teacher who didn't like her job or the students, which couldn't have been farther from the truth. I just couldn't find ways to make "I love my students and they love me" into funny jokes. It was much easier to write, "I was a teacher for many years. There were a lot of death threats. And the parents didn't like me making 'em." Or, "I have a solution for getting smaller class sizes: Get rid of those crosswalks. *(Pause while the audience realizes I'm implying not all kids will survive crossing the street.)* Smart kids'll figure it out. State test scores will shoot way up!"

There was one joke I told about the boys in my class who wouldn't behave. The joke was completely fictional. But after the show, three women rushed up to me. They were moms of boys in my class. I thought, *Oh no, here it comes. They're going to complain to the superintendent tomorrow, and I'll have no teaching position to go back to at the end of my leave.* Instead, the moms raved about my set, and bragged to the people around them that I had been talking about THEIR sons! (I hadn't.)

On stage at my home club, Harvey's Comedy Club

CHAPTER 7

WHO AM I?

It's said that it takes about ten years of experience for a comedian to finally find their "voice" or their true stage persona. That struggle between trying to be funny and edgy, while still remaining true to myself took years. I really didn't know who I was, on or off stage. It was kind of like I was a teenager again, trying to figure out life. I enjoyed going to the far edge of "acceptable" for a change. It was fun to be in some bar in some town in the middle of nowhere, making people laugh with my raunchy material.

Something completely unexpected began to happen, too. I had been "invisible" to men for the last twenty-one years of my life, having been cloistered away in a classroom. But after the shows, men from the audience would come talk to me, offering to buy me drinks. I never accepted, but I admit it felt good to be noticed. Perhaps the reason I was suddenly being noticed was that my raw material made people think I was loose. Maybe another woman would feel offended, but I wasn't. This new kind of attention was unexpected and fun. It was exciting to be the center of attention.

The added attention gave me more confidence, too. I began entering more comedy competitions. In September 2007, I entered the San Francisco Comedy Competition, and in

November, the Seattle Comedy Competition. Being the comedian with the least amount of experience in each of these contests, I had no illusions to make it past the preliminary rounds. In San Francisco I took 4th place on one of the nights in front of a huge crowd. I didn't fare as well in Seattle, taking an embarrassing last place for the week.

Did that mean I should roll up into a little ball and die? Or quit? It meant I had to keep working. Giving up easy wasn't my style. Nearly every night I'd either be at an open mic or a paid gig, working on my material and delivery. When Andre Paradise's annual Shades of Laughs Competition came around again, I competed once more. This time I was a finalist.

Probably the competition that was the most fun, though, was the Bay Area Black Comedy Competition in northern California. I was the first white female comedian to be accepted into the competition. Thanks to all those gigs I did for Andre' Paradise, I knew how to perform for urban audiences. I didn't make it to the finals, but I definitely rocked the house. My hard work was paying off.

Which is why I asked for another year of unpaid leave from teaching.

CHAPTER 8

ROAD COMIC

Things really started to happen in my third year of comedy, my second year of unpaid leave. I was getting better at finding gigs. Before my teaching career, I had been a news producer at KGW-TV. In the newsroom I'd learned that people would take your call and put you through to the top if you talked to them on the phone with an air of credibility and confidence. So I made sure to sound confident when I called comedy club owners and booking agents all across the USA and Canada, assuring them that they'd be glad they booked me. I was also prompt about sending them a DVD with clips of my performances, in a time before press kits were sent electronically. Of course, once I got the booking, I also had to be able to back up my words. I always got asked back.

I spent five consecutive weeks on the road in the Midwest, performing in the very clubs on the same stages where Ellen DeGeneres, Jerry Seinfeld, George Carlin, Jay Leno and many other greats performed. I'd look at their pictures on the walls of the club and feel so lucky to get to perform there too.

Several different venues booked me in Atlanta, where I spent a week. To my surprise, one of my sets even ended up being posted on Rooftop Comedy on the Internet. I also featured runs in North Dakota, Utah, Idaho, Arizona, Texas, Pennsylvania, Virginia, New Jersey, and thirty other states.

Lancaster, PA

Newport News, VA

Princeton, NJ & Reno, NV

Erie, PA

New York City, NY

El Paso, TX

Las Vegas, NV

Pleasanton, CA

Pasadena, CA

Fort Wayne, IN

Sacramento, CA

Los Angeles, CA

Finding my way around the United States and Canada on my own definitely was good for keeping my brain working hard. I don't know how comedians managed to find their way back in the day using only road maps. I started out using MapQuest. I'd print the directions and try not to get in a wreck as I simultaneously drove and looked at the paper.

MapQuest wasn't always correct. I ended up in the middle of a cornfield in Iowa, twice, thanks to MapQuest. Fool me once, shame on MapQuest. Fool me twice, time to get a GPS.

There were plenty of unusual things to see wherever I went. Probably the craziest was an entire field of giant, white, concrete ears of corn in Dublin, Ohio.

Me, standing behind a giant white concrete ear of corn in
Dublin, Ohio

There were lots of other oddities, too. Here are some of them:

Catsup water tower in Missouri

Giant dog on hilltop in Nebraska

Giant bat and ball in Midwest

In the jaws of a shark in south Texas

Circle of giant urns in Ohio

Threesome in Duluth, Minnesota

Teapot gas station in Zillah, Washington

Smallest town ever! Kyburz, California

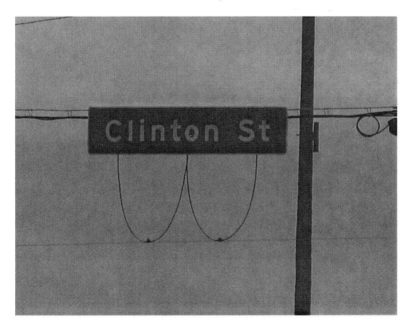

Suggestive wires in Ft. Wayne, IN

Amish highway sign in Pennsylvania

*While sleeping in my car somewhere in Illinois, I woke up to
the sounds of a cardinal looking at itself in my side mirror
for about ten minutes*

Comics sometimes have to deal with hecklers. A heckler is a person in the audience who yells out during the show. Sometimes they're drunk, but other times they're just an attention seeker. Heckling is usually unwanted by the comics because it disrupts the show. Most comics are good at shutting the person down immediately with a well-aimed insult or retort. I was not good at this. Thankfully, I didn't have too many hecklers.

My first heckling incident happened in Toledo, Ohio. I was the feature act at Connexions Comedy Club. The Thursday and Friday shows had gone really well. But on Saturday night, the audience just wasn't into it. The emcee had gotten tons of laughs the first two nights, but on this show he bombed. The guest act had also done well the previous nights, but he bombed too. I wasn't worried. I'd been doing comedy for a while now, and I figured I'd show these guys how it's done. That was mistake number one.

I confidently stepped on stage and said my first few lines, which always got laughs. "I used to be a teacher. That No Child Left Behind Law sucked. No child left behind, that was half the fun of going on field trips."

Nothing.

Then I made mistake number two. "Hey, guys, this is Saturday night! I thought you came to laugh!"

Some young guy in the back yelled, "We thought you'd be funny!"

The audience gasped and eagerly awaited my reply. I was stunned into silence for a moment that seemed like a lifetime as I tried to think of how to respond to that. The cocky confidence from a minute before was nowhere to be found. I had no idea what to say, no snappy comeback, no quick retort. Maybe he's right. Maybe I'm not funny. I looked down at the floor, trying to hide the tears that were welling in my eyes. *Don't let them see you cry. You've got to man up and keep going.* I had twenty-nine more minutes to fill.

"Um," I said quietly into the microphone, "I've been doing comedy for three years now. And I've always wondered what it would be like to get heckled. Now I know. It feels awful."

The audience laughed uncomfortably. Then I took a deep breath, and just went into my next joke as if nothing had happened. The audience politely laughed during the rest of my set, and I was never more relieved to get off stage. The headliner, Shane Mauss, then went up and KILLED. He showed me what a REAL professional does.

I learned so many lessons that night. I learned that every audience is different. I learned not to blame the audience if things aren't going well. I learned not to ever again be cocky. I learned that I'd better have a funny comeback ready if someone heckles me. I learned I'd better get a tougher skin. I learned what real class is because after the show Shane couldn't have been nicer or more understanding. His compassion toward me spoke volumes about him. Most of all, I learned that I had a LOT more to learn.

The next time I had a heckler was at my very first headlining gig. It was at Uncle D's Comedy Club in Spokane, Washington. The owner, Don Parkins, was taking a risk by booking me since this would be my first time headlining. I had an hour of material, though I can't say it was stellar. Being able to "fill an hour" means very little if you aren't getting laughs. Thankfully, I got tons of laughs. But a woman in the front row who'd clearly had too many margaritas was getting louder and louder. She wasn't trying to be rude; she just wanted attention. Often, drunks at comedy shows think they're "helping" the comedian by yelling out. They usually aren't. When she loudly announced she "needed to pee" and left to go to the bathroom, the audience and I shared a moment of relief that she was gone. She came back just as I was finishing my last joke, sixty minutes into my set. I got a huge laugh on my last punch line.

"Thanks so much, you've been a great audience!" I added, and began walking off the stage. But a waitress came running up to me and whispered, "We haven't passed out the checks yet! Don says you need to fill ten more minutes!" *WHAT????* Every joke in my repertoire had been used. I had nothing left to fill even one more minute, much less ten. I stepped back up on stage, trying not to look like a deer in the headlights while frantically trying to think of something to say.

The tipsy woman who had just returned from the bathroom yelled out, "Yaaaay, you're back!" Never have I been happier to have an annoying drunk in the audience.

"Aaaaaand you're still here, too...." I said, feigning disappointment.

The audience died! That woman and I bantered back and forth while the audience egged us on for nearly ten minutes. She saved me! Don invited me back to headline several more times after that successful first set.

My name up in lights at Uncle D's Comedy Club in Spokane, WA

It was an amazing third year all right. Remember how I said that comedians usually don't headline until they've been featuring for at least five years? I was now getting offered headline spots in several clubs across North America, after only three years since my very first open mic. I'm the first to admit that I was not truly ready to headline. No matter how hard you work, you truly don't know what you're doing just three years in. But while other beginning comics might get on stage once every week or two, I had been out there nearly every night of those first three years, learning and soaking in everything. I figured, if someone was willing to take a chance on me, why not go for it? I doubted that other comics in my place would have turned down these opportunities either. It didn't occur to me that if I bombed as the headliner, comedy audiences might not return to the club, which would cost the club owner money.

The fact that I, a relative newbie, was getting to headline clubs, did not sit well with a couple comics whom I barely knew. In fact, they actively tried to prevent me from getting booked. I was told by club owners and booking agents that these two veteran comedians had advised them not to book me. I never confronted the comics. I figured the best revenge would be to just keep getting better and getting more gigs. The good news is that the club owners always asked me back to headline again.

And then came the opportunity of a lifetime.

CHAPTER 9

IRAQ

It was January 2009. I was well into my third year of stand up comedy when I was given an amazing opportunity: To go to Iraq and Kuwait to entertain our troops. I had never supported the war, but I jumped at this chance to go overseas. I wanted travel, adventure, and to put this prestigious credit on my comedy resume'.

As I would learn, I was going for all the wrong reasons.

I went to Iraq with ignorant, naïve opinions that I had held for all of my adult life. Coming home, I was a changed person, with huge respect for the men and women serving our country.

This is my diary from this life-changing journey to Iraq and Kuwait:

DAY ONE:

I'm at Dulles International Airport in Washington D.C. on a seven-hour layover. Plenty of time to talk to the soldiers who, like me, are waiting for the flight to Kuwait. I show my itinerary to the group of Marines sitting near me.

"It says I'll be at about ten different 'FOBS'. What's a FOB?" I ask.

The guys laugh. One of them explains, gently, as if imparting news that might be hard to take. "Well, it's like this: Over here," he gestures with his right hand, "is the big, safe military base. And way over here," he gestures with his left hand, "are the bad guys. YOU...are going to be...here." And he moves his right hand close to his left hand.

Turns out "FOB" stands for "Forward Operating Base", and I'm going to be performing for troops who don't usually get entertainment because they're located so close to enemy territory. Well...I said I wanted an adventure.

DAY TWO:

The twelve-hour flight from D.C. to Kuwait went quickly. I'm excited as I step off the plane and into the Kuwait International Airport. I run to the counter, grab a number, and wait to be called to pay for the paperwork to enter the country.

A soldier walks past me, shoulders slumped, looking like he's just lost his best friend. I'm over here to entertain the troops, I think. Now is as good a time as any to start. I catch his eye and ask, "Hey, are you okay? Is something wrong?"

"Some Christmas vacation," he replies, glumly. "I get home, and I'm presented with divorce papers."

My first introduction into what real life is like for a soldier. I want to console him. I offer words of sympathy, but all I can really do is stand and keep him company.

Two hours later, the other two comedians, Davin Rosenblatt and Dennis Ross, both of whom I've just met, and I are being driven to Arifjan Base, followed closely by two armed Marines in an escort car. Davin and Dennis are from the East Coast, and their luggage didn't arrive with them. I'm grateful mine did. I had packed lightly: one small carry-on and a small backpack for ten days of travel. The most precious item in my luggage is the chocolate. I packed three giant Mr. Goodbars, a big bag of peanut butter M&Ms, and a bag of Kit Kat miniatures. I might be sleeping in a tent, trudging through mud, or freezing cold at night, but as long as I have chocolate to see me through the tough times, I can survive.

DAY THREE:

At Camp Arifjan in Kuwait, we're finding that maybe things aren't as tough as we had expected them to be. The troops have two HUGE fitness centers, each the size of a football field, with all brand new state of the art exercise equipment, giant flat screen television monitors to watch the Armed Forces Network (AFN), racquetball courts, basketball courts, tennis courts and baseball diamonds outside.

They have a nice dining facility (D-FAC) where we have unlimited food choices; nice buffet dinner, or fast food, or sandwiches to order, free Baskin-Robbins ice cream. I'm amazed at how much money was put into this base – and then find out that the Kuwaiti government pays for it all.

This afternoon, we're driven to Ali Al Salem Base, about an hour away from Arifjan. The Army National Guard troops from Hawaii are our hosts. In spite of their being half a world away from where they grew up, they welcome us with such graciousness and warmth. They bring us what must be treasured gifts from their own families back home, like chocolate covered macadamia nuts that would be hard to get here in Kuwait. We share jokes and laughter, and even play a game of Scrabble before the show. During our Scrabble game in the MWR (Morale

Welfare Recreation) Center, other soldiers play pool, ping-pong, watch a movie, or wait in line to get on the bank of computers to email home.

A few hours later, our first show begins. There's an outdoor stage with a huge camouflage backdrop. I'm standing up there, looking out at fifty or sixty soldiers, trying to hide the fact that I'm scared to death. What if they don't like my jokes? What if they were hoping for somebody famous: I'm no Ellen DeGeneres or Wanda Sykes. What if they'd prefer a young, hot beauty queen? I'm middle aged. In fact, I could be their MOM. I crack my first joke, saying something about how I feel like I'm Bing Crosby in the movie "White Christmas" when he's in the battlefield singing to the troops. They all stare up at me with blank expressions. These men and women are in their early twenties, too young to know what the heck I'm talking about. Great. So I do my regular material. And they laugh. A lot.

Performing outside in Kuwait

Reminded me of White Christmas scene

At the end of my set, I take out the piece of notebook paper I've brought from home. "Before I left Portland, Oregon, I asked people what they would like me to tell the troops. They all told me to tell you 'thank you' and that they realize what you are sacrificing by being over here. They want you to know they're grateful for the fact that you're making it possible for all of us to have our freedom. And they told me to give you a hug from them. So after the show, if you want, I can give you that hug."

Afterward, the emcee tells the troops that the comedians will be available for autographs. I choke on the water I'm drinking. Autographs? Who would want MY autograph?

It turns out that LOTS of these young men and women not only want my autograph, but they want a picture too. They also indulged in that promised hug, which I thought they never would actually want. Turns out, they NEED that hug.

DAY FOUR:

Yesterday's visit to <u>Ali Al Salem Base</u> opened my eyes. The men and women stationed here may have a few amenities like fast food places and fitness centers, but the one thing they don't have is "home". Whether my jokes are funny or not, it seems my presence here is giving some of these great people a much needed respite from their feeling of isolation and homesickness.

Something else makes me glad I was chosen to be a part of this comedy tour. Several female soldiers come up to me after the show to thank me specifically for providing entertainment for THEM. They say a lot of the entertainers they get are beauty queens, cheerleaders, and misogynistic comedians. That's fun for the guys, but not all that fun for the female soldiers who need entertainment too. I guess I fit the bill for them, and I am so grateful I have this opportunity to do so.

We're given three hours' sleep. Then we rush to get on the big C-130 cargo transport plane. I'm wearing a heavy Kevlar flak vest, an ugly green helmet, and I'm sitting in this hollowed-out plane, knee-to-knee with the other two comedians, a hundred soldiers and private contractors. We're packed in like sardines. They all sleep, but excitement keeps me awake.

Helmet and Kevlar vest on the C-140 transport plane heading from Kuwait to Iraq.

Ninety minutes later we're in Iraq at the biggest U.S. base there: <u>Balad</u>. It looks like a small brown/gray concrete city. No green anywhere, except for a tiny patch of grass that somebody took the time to water every day.

We tour the base hospital. Everything is state-of-the-art at this emergency facility: Nothing but the best in equipment and personnel. The doctors tell us that if a soldier is brought to them within an hour of being injured, there's a 97% chance the soldier will recover.

I hear the screams of a small child. It's an Iraqi toddler, the victim of a house fire due to indoor cooking. The child's mother hadn't understood that she was supposed to change the bandages regularly, and now they have to be peeled off while the child suffers excruciating pain. Local Iraqi people come here for emergency medical aid. Part of America's commitment to helping them. They have nowhere else to go.

The hospital tour ends in the wing where a group of our soldiers wait to be flown to Germany for further medical treatment. They won't get to come to our show tonight. We want to perform for them, or talk to them, do anything for them that will help them feel better. It feels awkward. They're watching a movie, and we don't want to interrupt them, but yet it feels like some of them want to be interrupted.

So I just blurt out, 'Hi guys! Hi ladies! We don't want to interrupt your movie, but we just wanted to say hello." That breaks the ice, and some answer. I ask where they're from. Montana, Texas, Colorado, all over the U.S. We chat, but it's a struggle. One guy from Montana asks if I'll write back to him if he emails me. "Sure! Of course! Here's my email address!" He sends me a short email right that very minute, while we're still there. He is skeptical that I will really write back to him.

The nurse in charge says our time is up. She whispers apologetically that most of these wounded soldiers are pretty drugged up right now.

That night, I email the injured soldier from Montana. We still stay in contact to this day.

DAY FIVE:

We're rousted out of bed early because we don't want to miss our C-130 transport plane to the next base. What I soon learn, though, is that in the military the motto is "hurry up and wait". We get to the base airport, where we're told we have a 90-minute wait. Suddenly the power goes out. We sit in the dark. I talk to a Navy sailor. It's amazing how quickly friendships are made, and sad to know you may never see each other again.

Our plane arrives and we're flown to the next base, Telefar, which is out in the middle of the desert. We exit the plane and it flies back out again. Oddly, no one is here to greet us. The three of us stand there not knowing what to do. We go inside the nearest building, which turns out to be the mess hall. We tell the soldier inside that we're the comedians. Blank looks. They haven't heard anything about any comedy show. Apparently we've been dropped off here by mistake. No one knows what to do with the three comedians. So some of the soldiers show us around, and entertain us by letting us hold their M4 rifles, while another one calls in to headquarters for further instructions.

One of the soldiers let me hold his rifle. Not sure how I feel about this.

At last a Blackhawk helicopter arrives, and we run to it, climb on board, and it whisks us away to another base. It's cold in the chopper. The sides are open with a soldier at each window, hands on the triggers of their machine guns, ready to shoot. We're shadowed by another Blackhawk helicopter, also with two gunners. I feel scared that we're a target, and yet also calm, because I trust these men and women to protect us.

We were flown base to base in Iraq on Blackhawk helicopters, with doors wide open.

We fly low over the desert. I see the bombed out hovels and tiny clay-like villages. My heart aches for the people who lived there, and possibly died there. This is real. This is the awful result of war. This can never be made right.

As I look at the terrain, the Tigris River, the sand, I can't help but marvel at where I am. Not too long ago I was in the classroom teaching my seventh grade students about Mesopotamia, Sumeria, Babylon, and here I am, flying over that very region. It's easy to picture this looking exactly the same thousands of years ago.

We arrive at <u>Meraz Base</u>, near the city of Mosul. The seriousness of the war is evident everywhere we look. This base has been heavily bombed. The dining hall was destroyed a few years ago. We pass a memorial to the twenty soldiers killed in that onslaught. We're told that just three weeks ago, on Christmas Day, ten more bombs were dropped on this base. Worse, on New Year's Eve two weeks ago, a soldier was killed when a bomb dropped into the airport. The shooters were soon found and killed. How did our soldiers find them? Easy. A huge blimp floats over the town of Mosul. Inside that blimp are video cameras with telephoto lenses that can zoom in close enough to read someone's dog tag. Wow. I guess Big Brother really does exist and he's our military. Those cameras are monitored at all times, making it easy for our guys to see where the bomb originated. This is one time when I'm glad to have "Big Brother" watching.

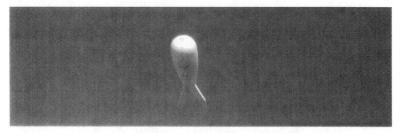

The blimp with cameras stationed overhead

We're escorted to our living quarters. I'd be lying if I said I wasn't a little scared to be here. But they tell us our bunks are in the most protected area in all of Iraq. Not because we're anything special, but because some Army general was recently here. We go through a maze of towering concrete walls topped with barbed razor wire. Along the way, we pass several bunkers fortified with green sand bags, and I make a note of where I will run and take cover if I have to.

One of the many bunkers near where I stayed on base

The show is a big success, and the troops really seem to want to talk afterward as we're signing autographs. A few men and women give me their email addresses, and I promise to write to them.

The brave firemen of the Mosul Fire Department didn't get to see the show, so we go to their workplace and spend some time talking and laughing with them.

It's now nearly midnight. As I walk to my bunk, a full moon lights the way. The air is crisp and clear. I look up and see a thousand stars, and am surprised to see Orion. He looks the same here as he does in my Oregon sky. That gives me comfort.

But then I hear a bomb go off in the distance, and I run to my bunk. As I lie on the thin mattress, I think I hear machine gun fire, too. Amazingly, though, I'm unafraid. Our military has me covered. These men and women do their jobs under duress every single day and night, and I am grateful. No matter what I think of the war, or our country's reasons for being and staying here, I can't deny that I owe a huge debt to the courageous people who are here to serve.

[Note: A few weeks after my return to Portland, the news media reported that four soldiers were killed by a roadside bomb near this base at Mosul. I felt terrible for the victims, and was also worried sick that it could have been some of the soldiers I'd met there, because they hadn't emailed me in days. At last I heard from them. One man, Jocephus, said he'd just come back from the bombsite, filling in the hole and re-paving the road where his fellow soldiers had just been killed.]

DAYS SIX - TEN:

Many people think Iraq is a hot oven all year. It's not. It can snow in the winter, and it definitely felt cold enough to snow last night here at **Meraz Base** near Mosul. The heater in my bunk just couldn't do the job, and the one thin blanket supplied didn't help much. During the night I put on my winter coat over my clothes, added gloves, a muffler, two pairs of socks, and leggings. When I awake this morning, I'm shivering. I'm staying in the VIP quarters. I can only imagine how cold the soldiers must be.

Over the next four days my two comedian cohorts and I ride on Blackhawk helicopters to seven more bases, doing our best to make the brave men and women there forget for an hour that they are in harm's way.

There are no women at **JSS Love Base,** however. This is a small outpost, far away from any of the larger bases. Fifty guys come in to the primitive wooden structure for a lunch far more basic and drab than what the guys at the bigger bases get. They sit on benches at long tables and wait for us to perform. These are young guys, and the officer in charge suggests that I do my bluest (raciest) material. I do. Big mistake. I get a few laughs, but it just isn't going as well as my earlier shows. I've chosen the wrong jokes, and I'm failing miserably. I feel horrible that I haven't given them a show that would make them laugh hilariously. Too late, I realize that these young soldiers see me as their mom, aunt, maybe even their grandma. They don't want to hear raunchy material from me. After my set I go to a little room behind the lunch area where no one can see me and cry silently. Shame washes over me. I've let these guys down, let the other comedians down, let myself down. I didn't do my job well. As a comedian, you win some, you lose some, and each show you just get back up on that stage and try again. But here, these soldiers deserve nothing but wins and I feel terrible.

Thankfully, the other two comedians, Davin and Dennis, are both huge hits. Their acts give me time to pull myself together, wipe away the tears, and put on a smile for the autograph session after the show.

As the men file by, I give each one a hug, and thank them for their service. In the helicopter on our way to the next base, Davin and Dennis try to console me, but I just feel terrible for letting those soldiers down.

All of the following shows go much better. We go to two or three bases each day, including **Brassfield-Mora Base,** where we go to the rifle range and shoot M4 rifles, M-240 machine guns, Saw machine guns, and a 50 caliber machine gun out of an armored truck. It turns out one of the soldiers in the truck is from the town in Oregon where I live! He even went to the same high school as my daughter!

Target practice.

New friends.

Later, we're honored to sit at a head table and have dinner with the soldiers before our show.

At **Normandy Base** we perform on an outside stage as helicopters fly overhead and drown us out with their noise. Now that's some serious heckling!

Woodcock Base is named after a young fallen soldier. The officer in charge shows us a huge map of the nearby Iraqi town and pinpoints the exact neighborhood where insurgents are living.

At **O'Ryan Base,** five Iraqis come up to me as we're leaving and gently grab me, excitedly saying, "Yellow, Yellow, Yellow," referring to my blond hair, and signal that they want to have their picture taken with me.

The Command Sergeant Major greets us at **Summerall Base,** and lets us try our hand at shooting an AK-47 and a 9mm Baretta before we go inside and perform for his four hundred soldiers.

We spend our last night in Iraq at Freedom Rest on **Speicher Base.** This is a place where soldiers who are completely stressed out, who are in need of a break in a huge way, can come for a brief respite. Waiting for me are two emails from soldiers at JSS Love, the base where I felt I had failed. One of the soldiers writes that he appreciated my coming to their base and that he really needs someone to talk to, and would I please write to him? The other email is from a soldier who says he appreciated the hug I gave him after the show, and that the hug had come at a time when he really needed it. My heart is filled, knowing that I had meant something to some of those men, and had helped them in some way after all.

We are tired, but we don't want to go home. We're supposed to have this last night off. Instead, we arrange to put on an extra show, specifically for the Blackhawk helicopter pilots, gunners, crew, and their entire brigade. It's our best show yet.

BACK HOME IN PORTLAND:

My journey to Iraq ended all too quickly. I would go again in a heartbeat. Ten days earlier, I had boarded a plane heading across an ocean to a war zone intending to have an adventure. I discovered something far greater. The men and women of our United States Military put their lives and families on hold to be over there. Whether we agree with why they were sent there, or why their orders are to remain there, the fact is they ARE there, serving with courage, humility, and valor. They deserve nothing but our utmost respect and gratitude. From the bottom of my heart, I thank them all, and I thank their families back home who wait with open arms for their safe return.

CHAPTER 10

CRAZY GIGS

I was now well into my comedy career, and had already experienced some of the most amazing, challenging, adventurous, memorable, exciting, scary, unpredictable, unexpected, and hilarious moments of my life.

Take, for instance, some of the crazier venues where I'd performed. I'm not talking about the many fine comedy clubs, casinos, military gigs, and colleges that have booked me. I mean places where I never would have guessed I'd be performing.

BIKER BAR: I was a little scared at first...until I discovered that rough looking guys and gals in tattoos and leather need to laugh as much as anyone else. They all were very welcoming in fact.

SWINGERS CLUB: I have to admit, I'd been curious about what it would look like inside a place where people enjoy a different "lifestyle" and like to "play". I expected amazingly gorgeous women and superbly handsome men, but it turned out most of the people looked pretty much like me...except I wore a lot more clothes. What a letdown.

36,000 FEET HIGH: I was invited to do ten minutes of my act while flying on Southwest Airlines from California to Oregon. The great thing about this was that no one could walk out if they didn't like my jokes.

HEAD SHOP: Tommy Chong was going to be at the grand opening of a store in Vancouver that sells things that people like to use at 4:20 in the afternoon. I was asked to perform for the huge crowd while they waited for Tommy to make his appearance. It wasn't much fun for me. Nobody could focus and they kept wandering off to Taco Bell.

STRIP CLUB: Puh-leeeeze. Why on earth would anyone in their right mind hire a middle-aged, plain looking female comedian to tell jokes in a "gentlemen's club" while the strippers go on break??? I was fully clothed, but felt naked standing next to that brass pole that was too small for me to hide behind. The men weren't any more thrilled that I was there than I was, but I will say that the strippers were the most supportive audience I've ever had!

APPLEBEE'S: Of all the strange gigs I've done, this one was the worst. Wholesome, tame, Applebee's. The regional manager wanted to see if having a comedy night in the bar area would be a good thing. It wasn't.

MAXIMUM SECURITY PRISON: I performed for one hundred and fifty black male inmates. I made no jokes about soap in the shower or captive audiences. They told me I was "off the chain" (that's a major compliment) and brought me back two more times.

CHAPTER 11

ONE DOOR CLOSES AS ANOTHER DOOR OPENS

My second leave of absence from teaching was over in the blink of an eye. The district didn't offer three-year leaves. So I had to make a decision to either go back to teaching or leave my job permanently to continue being a full-time comedian.

It wasn't a decision to be made lightly. For one thing, I still loved my job and I was at the top of the pay scale in my teaching career. As a comedian, I was barely breaking even, even though I was getting lots of headline spots.

I was determined not to take money from my husband's paycheck or our savings account to pursue this dream of mine. I hadn't had to yet, and the money situation hadn't been scary so far. I knew I could just go back to teaching at the end of the leave if I chose to.

What I hadn't counted on was loving comedy so much, or being so successful in finding gigs, low-paying as they were. Should I do the safe and sane thing and go back to teaching? Or should I jump over the comedy cliff without much of a parachute?

One thing was certain; my memory was getting much better since embarking on the new career. Writing new material, memorizing it, performing it, and navigating my way around North America by myself were all proving to be excellent brain workouts. This had all started because of my fear of dementia, hadn't it? Why quit now?

On the other hand, was I being selfish? Following my dream at the expense of my household income and time with my husband? After all, Clint never went on the road with me. He had to stay home and go to work. Even if he didn't have work, he didn't show much interest in coming along with me. And if it meant a flight, his airfare would have been an added expense.

The terrible economy solved my dilemma. Our school district was having huge budget problems, so they began offering teachers a chance to retire early. Instead of requiring us to wait until age fifty-eight or later, they began allowing teachers to retire at age fifty-five. I was fifty-four, but would turn fifty-five halfway through the school year. This meant I could go back to teaching for five months, then head back out on the road, secure in the knowledge that my pension would be there as a backup if I needed it.

So on January 29, 2010, I celebrated my fifty-fifth birthday, said a permanent goodbye to my teaching career, and hit the road again.

CHAPTER 12
SHE SLEEPS IN HER CAR??!

When you're on the road, finding a place to sleep on the nights when there isn't a show is a challenge.

Bookers and clubs usually only provide lodging on the nights you have a show. But if you can't find more gigs for the off-nights, you are left to your own devices to find a place to stay.

Even the cheapest fleabag motel is going to drain $40 a night out of your earnings. Multiply that by five, and you could spend $200 for lodging on the non-show nights each week. Add to that the cost of car rental, gas, food, and airfare, and it doesn't take a math whiz to figure out that a feature act making $100 per show is going to have a tough time covering expenses. I felt lucky if I managed to break even!

On one of my first big trips, to Iowa and North Dakota, I thought I'd be creative in finding a way to not have to spend money on a hotel. I went on Craigslist and asked if anyone would be willing to let me sleep on their couch for one night. I got five replies, and accepted one from a guy in his early thirties who didn't seem like an axe murderer. We agreed to meet that evening in the parking lot of a local mall in Iowa City at 8pm. But when the appointed time came, he didn't show up. A few days later, he sent an email saying he had chickened out. Maybe he was afraid *I* might be an axe murderer. Would've been nice if he'd TOLD me that night that he was taking back his offer of a place to stay; I waited around until 10pm, and finally drove on to Cedar Falls, where my show was scheduled for the next night. I figured I was probably better off not staying at some stranger's place anyway. (Ya think?!) I drove past the Cedar Falls city limits at 2:30am, and hoped the hotel where I was booked the following night would admit me early. No go. They were full up, and didn't even have a lobby for me to wait in. It was the middle of winter. The ground was covered with a couple feet of snow. What was I doing to do? I remembered passing an all-night diner as I'd driven into town, so I went back there and killed time as long as I could. I wasn't hungry, but I knew I had to order something. Nothing sounded good, so I ordered the strangest thing on the menu, deep-fried dill pickles. They tasted awful. The minutes seemed to crawl by. Thankfully, the waitress was friendly and understanding of my predicament. At 4am I finally went out to my car and tried to sleep. I felt like an idiot, out there in the parking lot of the diner just sitting in my car. Plus, it was freeeeeezing! I kept waking up every twenty minutes or so, shaking, turning the car heater on for a few minutes to warm up.

It wouldn't be the last time I'd sleep in my car.

Here's the routine: fly to wherever I had a few weeks of shows lined up, pick up my rental car, and drive to Walmart to buy a $5 blanket and a $3 pillow. Park in the far end of the Walmart lot or in a well-lit rest stop so that a restroom will be available. Stay in the driver's seat with keys in the ignition for a quick warm up or fast getaway if needed. Recline the seat. Pull the blanket up over my head so that passersby won't see that I am a woman.

"No, Sharon!! That's dangerous!!" I can hear you screaming in horror. Well, here are some other places I've tried:

* Sometimes other comics will let you sleep on their couches. Which would be great, if they weren't mostly bachelors...who apparently have a lower gag threshold than I do when it comes to cleanliness. I'm actually not all that picky, but a bathtub ring is one thing. A totally gray bathtub that's supposed to be white is another. On another note, using a back issue of Penthouse for toilet paper just seems creepy.

* In Wichita, I met a sweet, well-dressed elderly woman in a park who kindly invited me to sleep on her couch. I thanked her repeatedly, telling her how grateful I was for her kindness and generosity. I drove her to her home, which was in a very nice middle-class neighborhood. The exterior of her home looked well kept and tidy. She unlocked the front door and invited me to follow her in. I took one look and was aghast. She was a hoarder! It took everything I had not to turn and run. But how could I? It would be so rude after all of the gratitude I had shown her earlier. I stepped in. The stench of dog poop from a pet that wasn't potty trained was overpowering.

She cleared off a place on the couch and put a clean sheet on it for me. Then she said, "Now don't you mind about the mice. The lady across the street found twelve mice in her kitchen yesterday. And just this morning there was a big ol' mouse on that bag right there next to you. I clapped my hands at it, but it just stayed right there! They won't hurt you none, sweetie." I was awake all night, listening to the scuttling of tiny feet.

* I was smuggled onto an army base, so I could stay in the empty women's barracks for three nights. I was told to stay inside and stay away from the windows to avoid being seen. This was perfect, kind of like a writer's retreat, except for evading

national security and risking being thrown in jail if discovered.

* To kill time as late as possible in Topeka, I went to a tavern and played billiards for a couple hours. The married couple playing pool at the table next to mine offered to get me a hotel room and give me $100...if they could spend the night with me. Ew. No.

So you see? There could be worse things than sleeping in the car. Other than the obvious lack of safety, warmth, and a shower, the only bad thing that happened while spending the night in the car was the embarrassment of being awakened at 3am by a cop banging his flashlight on my window, asking me what the heck I thought I was doing.

It was a small sacrifice when following my dream.

CHAPTER 13

BACK TO IRAQ

In 2010, I was fortunate to be asked to go on a second tour of Kuwait and Iraq to entertain our troops. Unlike the cool January I had the first time, this one took place in the hottest time of year in August. It was 120-135 degrees the entire time I was there with co-headliners Lee Marvin Adams and Caroline Picard. This tour was just as amazing as the first one, and I have even more respect, if possible, for our military men and women now, seeing what they have to go through during the summer months!

We performed at Camp Patriot, Camp Victory, Camp Loyalty, Camp Ramadi, Al Asad, Camp Taji, JSS Muthana, Camp Hammer, JSS Duora, and JVS Palace for the Special Forces Unit.

On stage at Camp Taji, Iraq

Joking with a soldier on stage

Fantastic audience

Just as we were there to entertain them, our military hosts also entertained us. I got to steer one of their artillery speedboats in the Persian Gulf! They also showed me how to stop the boat quickly so the guys in the back would get drenched with seawater.

Our Navy guys in Kuwait were great hosts.

They actually let me steer.

If you stop the boat quickly...

...the guy in the back gets drenched!

On one of the bases in Iraq, the soldiers let us get inside one of the artillery tanks and drive it around a vacant lot for a few minutes.

It was a tight squeeze inside this tank!

We usually slept in the CHUs (Containerized Housing Units), which were kind of like makeshift trailers. Thankfully each CHU had an air conditioning unit, although one soldier told me his sometimes didn't work. The CHUs were surrounded and protected by tall concrete and sand barriers.

Containerized Housing Units

Protective barriers

We also got to spend four nights in one of Sadaam Hussein's eighty-eight palaces. Niiice. I had meals sitting at one of his lavishly ornate dining tables, sat on one of his thrones, and peed in one of his fancy toilets. At the time, it seemed fun. Looking back on it now, it just feels disrespectful. I know he did many horrible things, but what right did I have to be in his home?

Entryway to the palace

Ornate dining table

Fancy bathroom

While we were over there, all of the U.S. national news stations were headlining their evening newscasts with "Final Combat Troops Leave Iraq!" That was so hard for the service men and women in Iraq to take -- because 50,000 troops WERE STILL THERE serving our country. It was a matter of semantics. The troops were no longer called "combat" troops, but they were still there and didn't want to be forgotten. I know I will never forget them.

CHAPTER 14

UGANDAN SOLDIERS

The security guards doing sentry duty on most of the U.S. military bases in Iraq were Ugandan soldiers. At first I was afraid of them. Standing there with serious looks on their faces and machine guns in their hands, they looked very intimidating. But then someone told me to say "Jumbo jumbo" to the Ugandans. It means "Hello" in Swahili. I tried it, and was greeted with a huge smile, a happy "JUMBO JUMBO!" and a handshake in return.

The last base we visited was Camp Hammer. Several off-duty Ugandan soldiers stood in the back of the big meeting hall, watching our performance. They might not have understood everything we were saying, but they looked like they were enjoying the show. Afterward, when I gave my usual hugs to the servicemen and women who filed past, the Ugandans joined the line for a hug too. I also gave each of them an autographed picture with my Facebook address.

When a soldier is off duty in Iraq, there isn't much to occupy their time except to go to the base recreation center. There are lots of computers there, and the Ugandan soldiers made use of them. So when I returned to the U.S., I had several Facebook friend requests waiting for me from them. I accepted of course.

There are fifty-five tribes in Uganda, and each speaks their own tribal language. Being a former British colony, English is also spoken by those who've gone to school. Most of my new soldier friends were from the Banyankole tribe, and spoke Runyankole. There's no Rosetta Stone for Runyankole, so I asked each of my new friends to teach me words and phrases in their tribal language. One of Ugandans, Kato, wrote to me regularly via Facebook. As we got to know each other better we also Skyped often. We became good friends, and he invited me to come to Uganda to see his beautiful country when his Iraq tour of duty ended in five months. And so I did!

PART TWO

CHAPTER 15

OFF TO AFRICA

"DON'T GO, SHARON!!" *"Sharon, you're a fool to go!"* *"Africans hate white people, Sharon!!"* *"Seriously, Sharon, they will capture you and use you as a white sex slave before they murder you!"*

These were the warnings from several people back home, including some of my African-American friends. Some of these statements were made out of fear. Recent news stories reported that tourists and missionaries had been kidnapped in Africa. Some of the statements were made out of ignorance about Africa in general and Uganda specifically. I mean, the only thing many Americans know about Uganda is that the ruthless, violent dictator named Idi Amin ordered hundreds of thousands of people killed in his country back in the 1970s. The other picture many Americans have of Africa is what we see on the Save the Children ads, showing poor orphans covered with flies. To be honest, I didn't know much about Uganda either. I had to Google it just to find out exactly where it was located. It's a landlocked country in the east/central part of the continent, surrounded by Kenya, Rwanda, Tanzania, the Democratic Republic of Congo, and Sudan.

Having recently done two comedy tours of Iraq, a war zone for heaven's sake, I wasn't too worried about going to Uganda.

That is, until one of my friends begged me not to go. Her brother had been murdered a decade earlier while on an aid mission there. He and his wife and children had moved to an outlying village to drill wells for running water and build a school. One night while he and his family were asleep, three young men from the village broke into the house and killed him.

Another friend brought to my attention that just six months ago, Somali suicide bombers had blown themselves up in a rugby stadium in Kampala killing seventy-four people. Kampala, Uganda's largest city, is where I would be going.

Then news broke that five white women had been kidnapped and one white man killed in neighboring Kenya by Somali terrorists. Okay, now I had to admit I was becoming a bit apprehensive about going. My husband was not at all happy that I was making this trip. But then, he hadn't wanted me to go to Iraq either, and look what I would have missed out on.

Kato had invited me, and was even paying for all of my expenses except for my flight. Ever since my first paid gig five years earlier, I had been putting every penny I made into a special savings account. It wasn't a lot, but it was enough to pay for the flight. I'd been working hard my entire life. This would be a week with no work, just an amazing adventure. In AFRICA!

Kato assured me that my safety would be his top priority. He and another former soldier, Moses, would be by my side at all times when I wasn't at the hotel he arranged for me. *Besides*, I thought, *I could just as easily die at home by slipping in my own bathtub or waiting for Alzheimer's, right?*

So, in January 2011, I boarded the plane for a nine-day visit to Uganda.

CHAPTER 16

THE LONG JOURNEY

My journey began at 3:40am at the Portland International Airport. From there I flew to San Francisco, then to Chicago, and on to Brussels, Belgium. The three flights had taken nineteen hours so far.

The Brussels airport was scary, because I had no clue where to go or what to do, and I had no boarding pass for the last leg of the trip. Everyone was speaking French, and I couldn't understand what was being said. Fortunately, before disembarking the plane, I had heard the pilot say that passengers flying to Africa needed to go to Terminal T, wherever that was.

A long walk, a few wrong turns, and a bus ride later I finally arrived at Terminal T and boarded the plane for the final leg of my trip. I flew over the snowy French Alps, over the green South of France, over the blue Mediterranean Sea, and over the tan Sahara Desert. Ten hours later, I was thrilled to be landing in Uganda! Only.... I wasn't in Uganda.

Instead, we had flown to Rwanda for refueling. After another hour on the ground, we made the truly final leg of the trip, and arrived in Entebbe International Airport in Uganda.

I followed everyone as we walked across the tarmac and into the airport terminal to get in line to buy our visas. Another hour, and a $50 payment later, I had my visa in hand and headed toward the baggage area. The luggage still had not been unloaded. It would be another long wait.

At last I retrieved my bags and headed to the airport lobby, hoping Kato would be there to greet me. He wasn't. There were crowds of black men inside and outside the airport, wanting to be hired to carry luggage or for transport. I looked at their faces. No Kato.

So I went outside the airport, onto the entryway sidewalk. Maybe he would be there? Lots of young men eagerly stepped up to me, offering me taxi service. Still no Kato. Maybe he was in an accident? Delayed in some way? After that long, exhausting journey and the frustration of the long waits for the visa and luggage, this disappointment of not having Kato here to greet me was too much. Tear started streaming down my face. I tried hard not to panic. The men around me wanted to help. They took my phone and tried calling Kato for me, but my cell phone didn't work in Uganda. They offered to take me to a hotel, but I refused. I said I would stay at the airport until Kato arrived, because I *knew* he would come. I sounded more certain than I felt. I was on the edge of panic. What if he never showed up? What if this was all just one big hoax? What had I gotten myself into???

I tried to go back inside the airport, but the guard refused to allow me back in. Just as I was about to panic, I saw him! Inside the airport! Looking for me!

"KATO!! KATO!!" I yelled. He looked over and ran to me. We hugged joyously. This was really happening!

Kato introduced me to his best friend, Moses, and we walked over to the car that had been hired to pick me up. The driver, Cyrus, was waiting for us. Cyrus knew very little English.

It was now past midnight in Uganda, and we drove the thirty-five miles to Kampala in the dark. There were no freeway overhead lights. In fact, there was no freeway. Just a two-lane road, and some eerie kerosene lanterns or charcoal fires lighting roadside stands along the way. I was clearly not in America anymore.

CHAPTER 17

NILE AND SAFARI!

Kato was nearly six feet tall without an ounce of fat on his body. He had a high forehead, short dark hair, big brown eyes, and dimples in his cheeks when he smiled. He was twenty-five years old, but in some ways had the maturity of someone much older. He was serious and studious, and one could tell that he was going to go far in life. He was of the Banyankole tribe, and grew up with his very large family in central Uganda, near the town of Mbarara. His family raised ente, the Runyankole word for long-horned cattle. Kato spent much of his youth helping to herd the cattle before going to boarding school.

Moses was from the same tribe as Kato. He was shorter and a couple of years older than Kato, but seemed younger. He had a higher voice than I would have expected from looking at him, but this added to his charm. It was easy to make him laugh, and we quickly became buddies.

Kato and Moses

Kato, Moses, and the driver, Cyrus, escorted me everywhere for the next seven days. Kato had planned an amazing week for us. We took a lovely boat ride on the Nile, near the city of Jinja. We saw hundreds of butterflies and plenty of birds, including cormorants, egrets, and the giant kaloris, which look a bit like big storks with ugly gullets.

At the source of the Nile, near the town of Jinja

On the bank of the Nile River

Boating down the Nile River with Kato

Kato points to where Lake Victoria ends and the Nile River begins.

At Bujagali Falls, a native teenage boy rode down the dangerous rapids on a plastic yellow container called a jerry can. It looked like fun to me! He came up to me afterward, and I smiled and clapped. I was too ignorant to realize he was actually looking for tips for putting on a show for me. Kato told me later that this was probably how the boy supported himself. I felt terrible for not giving him a few shillings, which is the currency in Uganda.

Teenager riding jerry can down rapids.

Moses posing at Bujagali Falls

Dusk at Bujagali Falls

We went to the Entebbe Wildlife Reserve and saw lions, chimpanzees, giraffes, monkeys, crocodiles, exotic birds, and many other animals that had been rescued from poachers. The animals all seemed to be in good physical shape, although one of the chimpanzees across a moat from us kept looking at us forlornly, holding out his hand for food. At least he survived. Many animals in Africa aren't as lucky. Poachers are known to cut off rhinoceros' horns, which are ground to powder and sold as an aphrodisiac in China. Gorilla hands have shown up in exotic marketplaces, being sold as ashtrays. Elephants pay dearly with their lives because their tusks are made of ivory.

Rescued chimpanzee

Uganda's national bird, the crane, has a beautiful orange plume on its head

Afterward we went to Lake Victoria, where I briefly waded in the cool water. "Come on in! The water's fine!" I yelled to Kato, Moses, and Cyrus on the shore. For some reason, they wouldn't go in the water. It would be many months later when I discovered why.

On the shore of Lake Victoria, several camels wandered near us to snack on the bushes. We slowly approached them, and gently touched them. For the most part they ignored us, until one tried to kick Kato!

Dare I touch this wild camel?
Kato found out what would happen!

Near the end of the week, we went on a seven-hour car ride across the country to Queen Elizabeth National Park in western Uganda. We drove past village after village with low buildings and homes made from red mud bricks. We passed fields of tea, sugar cane, corn, and pineapple. We saw trees filled with papaya, mango, passion fruit and avocado. I imagined this might be what Hawaii looked like before it became crowded with tourists.

We stopped on the Equator. There was a monument where you could stand in both the northern and southern hemispheres at the same time.

Cyrus, Moses, and Kato on the Equator

Straddling the northern and southern hemispheres

Farther down the road we saw a young boy herding ente. Kato asked Cyrus to stop the car so we could get out. He told me that this is very much like what he used to do as a boy.

Ugandan boy herding ente (long horned cattle)

When we stopped for lunch, I got my first taste of matooke, the boiled bananas that most Ugandans eat regularly as their main dish. It was delicious!

Matooke

As we continued on to the far western side of the country, a couple of wild boars ran out in front of our car. Thankfully we avoided hitting them. We also saw giraffes in the distance, and a leopard only twenty feet away. I started to roll down my car window to take a picture. Kato and Moses screamed in unison, "NO!!!!" I quickly rolled it back up, as Kato explained that the leopard could easily jump into the car and attack us!

Wild leopard near our car (Picture taken with window rolled up!)

I was actually more worried about something else that could attack us. The U.S. State Department had issued a warning to all tourists to stay away from western Uganda, due to Congolese rebels. And yet, here I was, right where I wasn't supposed to venture.

We finally arrived at Queen Elizabeth National Park, where we boarded a safari boat. It took us down the Kazinga Channel, which separates Uganda from the Congo. We got close-up looks at herds of water buffalo, families of hippopotami and giant elephants playing in the water, a huge triangle of birds sunning themselves on a sandy beach, and two big crocodiles opening their jaws wide to show us their sharp teeth. Farther down the channel, some village women were washing clothes as children played in the water and waved to us.

Water buffalo

Hippopotamus with her baby

Birds sunning themselves

Crocodile with mouth wide open

Wild elephants grazing and playing by the water in the Kuzinga Channel

After this fun safari, I was tired and ready for a nice, relaxing drive back to Kampala. But Cyrus decided to take a different route this time, thinking it might be a shortcut. He was wrong. This decision resulted in a harrowing eight-hour nightmare of travel. Imagine driving on an unpaved, rocky road that has no shoulders and is just barely wide enough for two cars. You'd go slowly and cautiously, right? Not in Uganda! We, along with every other car on the road, seemed to be going forty-five to sixty mph. There were streams of traffic in both directions, no dividing lines down the middle, boda bodas (motorcycles) recklessly zipping in and out, and pedestrians and bicyclists on the edge of the road. Add potholes and speed bumps every hundred feet or so, high enough that the bottom of the car scraped on them. AND THIS WAS ALL AT NIGHT, WITH NO STREET LIGHTS, NO ROAD SIGNS, AND NO TRAFFIC SIGNALS!

The horrendous ride seemed to go on forever. Just when I thought things couldn't get any worse, I had to go to the bathroom. I hadn't gone since before lunch, and I realllllly needed to pee. At last there was a gas station up ahead. We stopped for gas, and

I asked to use the restroom. Um....restroom? What they had was a slab of cement in the back of the building, with three walls around it. There was no door. No privacy. No toilet paper. And no toilet. Just a slab of cement. It was slanted a bit so that pee could run downhill toward the back wall. I had on jeans, shoes, and socks. How was I going to do this???? I would have to take off my jeans and shoes and socks completely, or I would surely pee all over them. This was a desperate situation! Time was of the essence! If I didn't hurry up and get my clothes off, it would no longer matter! In the meantime, Kato came around the corner of the building to see if I was okay. I yelled at him to stay away, and to stand guard for me. I completed my mission without too much collateral damage, and got back into the car. By the time we finally made it back to the hotel, we all were exhausted. I was just grateful to have made it back alive, in one piece, with no encounters with Congolese rebels!

It rained on my final day in Uganda. The deep, wide gutters lining the streets filled up like dry riverbeds in a flash flood. It seemed fitting that it was overcast and gray because I was truly sad to be leaving. It had been an amazing, thrilling, adventure-filled week. Kato and Moses had been such great company, and wonderful protectors. I had brought two silver pieces from home that had a word stamped into each. I gave the one imprinted with "HUMOR" to Moses, because he had a silly sense of humor and was always making me laugh. I gave Kato the silver piece imprinted with "VISION" because I knew that Kato, with his intelligence and ambition, was destined for great things.

Kato, Moses, and Cyrus accompanied me to the airport. We all hugged, and I promised never to forget them. The Pearl of Africa, as Uganda is called, had filled my soul. I had to return someday.

Kato and I at the Wildlife Preserve

CHAPTER 18

BACK TO THE PEARL

After returning home, I began reading the online Ugandan newspapers and discovered that there was stand up comedy in Kampala! It was new, only about two years old. I went on Facebook and searched for the comedians mentioned in the newspaper article. I found a few of them and messaged them. Not only did they reply, but they invited me to perform with their troupe as well.

In one reply, the troupe manager, Kabuye, mentioned to me that he co-ran a charitable organization to help schoolchildren and elderly people in the village of Bbira. He sent me a link to a short video clip of some of the children playing. I immediately fell in love with them. Being a former teacher, I was drawn to the idea of going to the village and helping out at the school in any way I could.

I wouldn't have Kato or Moses to escort me this time, but that was okay. I liked the idea of doing this on my own. What better challenge for my brain?

I'd be in Africa for three months. I'd miss Thanksgiving, Christmas, New Year's Eve, and my birthday with my family. I had never been away from them for that long. But this was an opportunity I just couldn't turn down.

I knew the journey would be long as I boarded a plane in

Portland, Oregon on November 10, 2011. Had I known that ten extra hours would be tacked onto that due to mechanical problems, I think I would have looked for another airline.

I slept as much as I could on the long flight over the Atlantic Ocean, and practiced going through my homemade Runyankole language flashcards whenever I was awake. I was determined to arrive in Uganda at least knowing how to say polite phrases in one of their fifty-five tribal languages.

I finally landed in Entebbe, Uganda on Sunday morning, November 13, 2011, at the end of a forty-nine hour journey. Despite several reassurances from a myriad of airline staff, NONE of my luggage arrived with me. It would be six days before I finally had shampoo, deodorant, allergy pills, most of my clothing, and everything else that was in my suitcases that had been lost somewhere in the world. I made it though, and now the real adventure would begin.

CHAPTER 19

TANDEM HOTEL

After I had left Uganda nine months earlier, Kato went back to live on his parents' cattle ranch in central Uganda. Cell and Internet service were sparse there, and I didn't hear much from him. Moses, on the other hand, worked in Kampala. He and I were in contact often via Facebook.

I asked Moses to try to find an inexpensive hotel or apartment for me in the Kampala area. My only requirement was that it must have a real toilet, not a hole in the floor. He was having a hard time finding a place that filled that requirement. There were three or four fancy hotels in Kampala, but they were way out of my price range. The more affordable places didn't have toilets.

At last, Kato came to Kampala and helped in the search. He found a hotel in the Makindye district, just outside of Kampala. Not only did each room have a toilet and shower, the Tandem Hotel was located across from the Ugandan army base. The hotel had an armed guard, and the front gate was locked every night at 11pm. That should reassure my friends and family at least.

Kato, Moses, and Cyrus met me at the airport again. It was a happy reunion. We drove to Tandem Hotel so I could check in. The manager was a very tall, somewhat heavy man with a friendly smile and a deep, booming voice with laughter reminiscent of those old "Un-Cola" commercials. All of his employees called him "Manager". I came to privately refer to Manager as "Yes! Yes!" because that's what he always said when anyone approached him.

Tandem Hotel, in Makindye District

Manager

In Manager's small office, Kato helped with negotiations for payment. Kato was from the same tribe as Manager, so I was given a better price for my room than I might otherwise have gotten. I would be paying $22 a night. This would include a complimentary breakfast each morning in the dining area downstairs. He had done me a huge favor by finding this hotel for me. Unfortunately, he received word that night that his young teenage nephew had just died. He left immediately to go back to the family compound in Mbarara to help with funeral arrangements. It would be more than a month before I'd see him again.

I loved my room. It had a queen bed with mosquito netting hanging over it, a wardrobe with two drawers and a pole for hanging clothes, a television with a snowy picture and three or four channels, and a small bathroom that had a tiny sink, and a real toilet. It usually took about five flushes to get it to work effectively, but at least it wasn't a pit latrine! There was also a showerhead in the bathroom and a hot water heater located above the toilet. Water flooded the bathroom each time I took a shower because the drain was clogged.

Each morning I was awakened by the crowing of a rooster and the cawing of loud, crow-like birds called Mpaas. At first it was annoying, but I gradually began to look forward to these natural alarm clocks.

I'd get up, shower, and head down the two flights of stairs, greeting the hotel maid as I went. In the dining hall, Jolly, the waitress, brought my breakfast. I was given the same thing every morning: A plain omelette, plain toast, fresh watermelon and pineapple, and Ugandan hot chocolate. The omelette was always white, even though it wasn't an eggwhite omelette. The chickens are raised in cages and are so poorly fed that their yolks don't turn yellow.

I was fortunate to have Internet access at the hotel, although I had to go downstairs to the lobby or dining room to get a signal. I soon learned, though, that we would only have electrical power about four hours each day, thanks to the Ugandan government not paying its bill to the power company (UMEME). I didn't mind too much. I had brought a flashlight and candles, which came in handy every night when the power was out. Plus, with no electricity for my laptop or TV, I had even more reason to go out and meet people and explore my surroundings.

It turned out that most of the people where I was living were from the Baganda tribe. They spoke Lugandan, not Runyankole! So I needed to start learning this language, too. The first words I learned were, "Olli oyta" and "Webale nyo", which meant "Hello" and "Thank you very much." *Come on, memory, keep working.*

Next door to the hotel was a cafe with no indoor seating. It just had a covered patio with tables and chairs. On my second night, I heard a lot of cheering and yelling coming from the patio. I walked over to see what was going on. A television was mounted up near the rafters, and twenty or thirty young local men were watching the soccer game. Somehow UMEME was able to turn the power back on just in time for the soccer games.

It's pretty rare for white people to be seen in Makindye, especially white women with blond hair. I always got stares from everyone I passed. As I walked toward the café that evening, three young men sitting at a table smiled at me. I thought they looked friendly, so I smiled back and tried out my new phrase: 'Olli otya!' The men gasped in surprise. Apparently even more rare than seeing a white woman was hearing one speak their language. They invited me over. It was hard to understand their British/Ugandan accents, and I didn't understand any of their Lugandan. They had just as much trouble understanding my American accent. Their names were William, Michael, and Ben. Ben was the barber who worked in the barbershop adjoining the cafe. In Uganda they aren't called 'barbershops' though; they're called 'saloons'. Not salons. Saloons.

Soon a customer came for Ben. Ben invited me to follow them through the long strands of beads in the entryway to the saloon. I sat on a plastic chair against the wall, watching him shave the man's head. I couldn't tell how old Ben was. Twenty? Forty? His head was shaved. He was wearing slacks and a pink shirt, and had sort of a little giggle when he laughed. I wondered if maybe he was gay. If so, he wouldn't have been able to admit it openly. In Uganda, that could get a man killed.

Ben would occasionally look over at me and smile as he shaved the man's head. I knew I was going to like this guy. He just seemed like a man of good character.

Ben the barber (l) and his best friend Michael (r) on the café patio outside the 'saloon'

CHAPTER 20

TRAGEDY AND COMEDY

On the third day, Kabuye came to Tandem Hotel to meet me. He was the comedy troupe manager who had contacted me about helping the children in the village of Bbira. He was a tall, slender, quiet man. I was surprised at how young he was. He was just twenty-six years old.

Kabuye's story was a sad one. As is often the case in Uganda, his stepmother was excruciatingly cruel to him when he was a child. She beat him frequently and assigned him many hours of extremely hard manual labor each day. One day, when Kabuye was about ten years old, a strange man came to his village. He told all of the children that if they wrote letters, they would get sponsors and receive gifts and money from them. The children wrote the letters, but never received anything in return. Kabuye strongly suspects that the man who came to the village received the gifts and cash and kept them for himself.

Kabuye wanted to be a better example for the children of his village, and to truly bring them help and hope. He and his best friend, Twagala, created a charity called the Children & Elderly Support Organization (CESO). The charity was so new that the only things that had been done so far were weekly gatherings of the village children for lessons and creative play and dance.

I had a big suitcase filled with school supplies and gifts for the children at the village school, but my luggage was still lost. So

Kabuye decided we'd wait to go to the school until the suitcase arrived.

Instead, that night he took me to the nightclub where the comedy troupe performed. The venue was Effindy's and the troupe was called "Brain Wash". There were nine young black men in the troupe, all in their early twenties. Tumusiime, Arthur, Bright, Arnold, Ken, Dickens, Ronnie, Omukabete, and Lam Juice all welcomed me into their troupe immediately, with smiles, handshakes, and hugs. Before the show, we gathered behind the stage, swatting at mosquitoes and joking around.

Goofing around backstage with my new comedian friends.

The place was packed with local Kampalans. When it was time for the show to begin, I was surprised to hear the dance music volume turned up instead of down. Suddenly the comics grabbed my hand and moved me along with them. We all filed onto the stage, dancing as we went. Arthur, the emcee, called us to the front, one by one, where we each were expected to do a bit of a solo dance. I am NOT a dancer. Trying to not look too awkward, I smiled and moved a bit and got back into the line. Then we all went back stage again, and the comedy portion of the show began.

I was fourth in the lineup. On stage, I pretended not to know that Ugandans call white people "Muzungu".

"I'm so happy to be here in Uganda. Everyone is so friendly. You've even already given me an African name: Muzungu!"

Howls of laughter.

"Everywhere I go it seems like everyone already knows me. I walk down the street and all I hear is, 'Muzungu! Muzungu!'"

More laughter.

"And the men are so nice. They see me and yell, 'Muzungu! Can I have you?!' It's so sweet of them to want to invite me for tea!"

I was a huge hit that night. The Brain Wash comedians made me an official member of their troupe, and I became the first American ever to perform stand up comedy in Uganda.

CHAPTER 21

SCHOOL IN BBIRA

Six days after I arrived, my luggage finally showed up. I was so relieved. Not only were all of the things that I would need for myself over the next four months in one of the suitcases; the other was full of school supplies and gifts for the children in the village.

I had come prepared with lots of surprises for the children. Back home, I had asked two hundred of my Facebook friends to donate one dollar to help me help the children in Uganda. Unfortunately, only about thirty replied. But boy, did they come through! Their donations, along with generous donations from my family members, came to a grand total of $2000. Ten times what I had been hoping to raise! In addition to bringing the cash, I also brought a big suitcase filled with books, school supplies, and a bag of little toys and candy for each child. I planned to give them the bags for Christmas presents.

School supplies and books I brought in my suitcase for the children

Kabuye and I spent the morning in downtown Kampala, buying more school supplies and textbooks to add to the items I had in my suitcase. Then we headed out to the village, stopping along the way to buy beans, rice, maize flour, and salt for the school's food supply.

Village store where grains are sold

Measuring out the rice

Kabuye haggling prices

A worker helps carry bags to the car

When we arrived, children came running and cheering to greet us. They were so excited! A Muzungu had never come to their school or village before. I'm pretty sure they could tell that I was equally as excited to meet them! Some were carrying signs for me: *Welcome Sharon! Your coming is a blessing to us! It is a pleasure to receive you here! Fairly smoke the Ugandan atmosphere!*

I wasn't sure what that last sign was supposed to mean. Perhaps something about breathing in the fresh country air? No matter. It still translated to "Welcome" in any language.

"Olli otya!" I said to them, smiling.

They squealed and giggled in delight and replied, "Gende!"

"Kyebare ko?" I asked them the polite phrase meaning, "How are you?"

More giggles and smiles. "Kale!" they replied, which means, "Fine!"

The children ran to greet me.

They had been preparing for my visit.

The school had two mud brick buildings, each with two small classrooms. There were no doors in the doorways, no glass in the windows, and no desks. There were a few benches, but not enough for all of the children. They had no textbooks, no reading books, no school supplies. There were a few handmade charts on the wall, and a very old blackboard at the front of the classroom. Many of the sixty-five children who attended the school were orphans. They all needed clothing desperately: the shoes they wore appeared to be made of more holes than shoe. A few of the boys simply wore threadbare socks, and others just went barefoot.

The primary school in Bbira had two buildings, each with

two small rooms

The classrooms had no desks, only a few benches, and a blackboard

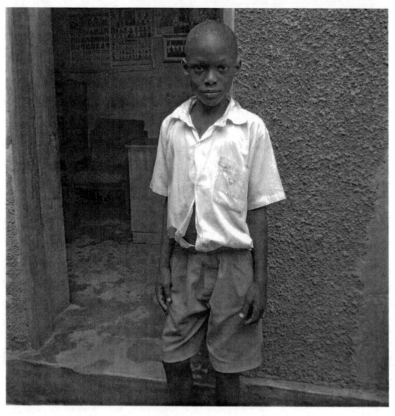

One of the students

The owner of the school was an elderly woman named Kate. She lived at the compound, and raised some of the orphans who went to the school. Twagala ushered me into Kate's living room so I could present her with the school supplies. She nearly cried with gratitude, continually shaking my hands.

"Madame Sharonee," she said, smiling, "webale nyo." I accepted her thanks and her hug. I loved the way some of the Ugandans pronounced my name with an "ee" at the end.

Showing Kate, the owner of the school, items I brought for the classrooms

Kate thanks me for the supplies while Twagala watches nearby

Next we all crowded into one of the classrooms. The youngest children, ages four to six, sat on the floor in the front row. Behind them, the seven to eleven year olds also sat on the floor. The oldest students, ages twelve to sixteen, had the privilege of sitting on the benches in the back.

The headmaster gave a very long welcoming speech. I was amazed at how long his speech went on, and even more amazed at how perfectly still and attentive the children were throughout the long lecture. Many American students might have started fidgeting and losing interest about five minutes into the speech. These students paid attention and remained still and silent till the very end.

After the speech, each grade level of students came to the front of the room and sang a song for me, some with dancing. The older boys accompanied the songs on big wooden drums covered in goatskins.

"Oh what a happy day, what a good daaaaaay,

What a happy daaaay, to see our dear Sharon!

We shall sing for you, we shall dance for you,

We shall shake-shake, shake-shake,

Oh what a happy day!"

"Webale nyo, nyo, nyo!" I delightfully thanked them after each song.

Students from each grade level sang for me.

The older boys accompanied on drums

Next came my gifts for the school:

* 300 ink pens and 100 pencils

* 100 spiral notebooks

* Primary and intermediate reading books

* 20 boxes of crayons and a few boxes of colored pencils

* Enough blackboard chalk to last a year

* Textbooks for the teachers, in English, Math, Science, and Social Studies for all seven grade levels

* Science and alphabet wall charts

* 2 pencil sharpeners to replace the bare razor blade they had been using

After the gift presentation, we went outside for a tour of the school. In addition to the four small classrooms, there was a small, closet-sized brick building in the back. It was the "kitchen", which consisted of a wood fire with a big pot hanging over it. Rice and beans would be cooked in this pot, or a maize porridge called *posho*. This is what the children ate for lunch each day. For some of them, it was the only meal they had all day. In the weeks to come, I would bring more big sacks of maize flour, rice, and beans to replenish the school's meager supply.

Next came the pit latrines. There were three narrow stalls – one for the boys, one for the girls, and one for the teachers. The headmaster opened one of the wooden doors, and I saw the hole in the concrete floor.

Adjacent to the pit latrines was the shower stall. It was simply a concrete platform enclosed by brick walls. No actual showerhead or running water. Just a yellow jerry can filled with water.

For playground equipment, the children had one old, flat soccer ball that had been borrowed from another school, and one ball made from plastic bags tied together.

Soccer ball made from old plastic bags

As we toured around the grounds of the school, the oldest boy, Mande, caught my attention.

"Madame Sharonee," he called to me.

"Yes?"

"Look at what I can do!" He did a funny "magic" trick with his hands, one that I had actually shown my own students back home. I applauded with appreciation.

"Mande, look at what I can do!" I said. I did the old trick of "cracking my nose." I bent my nose to the side and they heard the sickening sound of cartilage breaking. The trick was to keep my hands over my mouth to hide my thumbs. Then I clicked my thumbnails on my front teeth to make the sound.

Of course, everyone winced, thinking I had actually broken my nose. I took Mande aside and showed him how the trick was done. He caught on immediately and delighted the children several more times with the trick.

I asked Mande what he wanted to be when he grew up. "I want to be a lawyer. Or an artist. Or a comedian like you!"

There was something about Mande that set him apart from the others. Not just the fact that he was the tallest and oldest of the boys. Mande seemed to have this spark of curiosity about him along with a drive to be noticed, almost as if to say *Look at me. I need your help. Take a chance on me.*

At last it was time to go. The children gathered around me and gave me hugs. They had all captured my heart.

On the way back to Makindye, Twagala said, "Sharon, we'd like to give you an African name. You shall be called Nantongo." I loved the name, and was grateful for the honor.

The students show off their new writing books and pencils

The end of my first of many visits to the school in Bbira

CHAPTER 22

WHAT I LIKE ABOUT U...GANDA

As the days went by, I found so much to love about this country. I loved that there were no Starbucks, McDonald's or any other American businesses in sight. Finally, here was one place in the world where commercialism hadn't taken over.

The people were equally loveable. They were friendly and welcoming, especially when I smiled first and greeted them in their language. Most everyone dressed in business-type clothing. The men wore slacks, belts, dress-shirts, polished shoes. The women wore dresses, with their hair nicely done and their makeup applied beautifully. Everyone's clothing was clean and neatly pressed. This is especially impressive when you consider that many people don't have electricity, much less bathrooms with showers, a washer/dryer, or electric iron. It was explained to me that clothing is pressed by heating a non-electric iron filled with charcoal, or heated over a charcoal stove.

Iron being heated on charcoal stove

In comparison, I looked like a total slob, wearing my un-ironed jeans and casual tops. I did my laundry in two small plastic tubs on the floor of my hotel bathroom, drying it on a makeshift clothesline I strung across my room.

Washing clothes in my hotel room

Makeshift clothesline

Three weeks into my stay, I began to get a little homesick. It was Thanksgiving and I thought about my eighty-two year old dad, and my seventy-nine year old mom now in the middle stages of Alzheimers. Should I be half a world away, when each day my mom was losing more and more of herself? I sent an email to them:

Hi Mom and Dad,

Everything is going really well here. I'll be performing every week here with the Brain Wash troupe, PLUS I've been invited to perform on Thursday with another comedy group here. I can't wait!

Mom, I want you to know that you taught me something decades ago. When I was a toddler, I remember watching you wringing out the wet laundry before you'd hang the clothes up on the clothesline to dry at our house on 3rd Street. All these many years later, I am doing my own laundry by hand in my hotel room. Every time I twist a wet piece of clothing to wring out the water, I think about YOU and how you taught me this when I was just a tiny little girl. So thank you, Mom...you must surely know how much I appreciate you.

Dad, as I walk up and down the road here in Makindye, people wave and greet me. They know me because as I go on my walks, I smile and chat with them. Just like you always did in Cheney. So, thanks to what I learned from YOU, Dad, I have many friends here in my Uganda neighborhood. It is a great gift that you have given me.

I love you both.

Sharon

It was interesting how completely different the modes of transport were, compared to back home. People walked everywhere or rode in old white taxi vans that were meant to hold twelve people but usually carried sixteen or more.

Most people ride in affordable taxi vans

Usually crammed in tight, no AC

There were only two stoplights in all of Kampala, no lines in the road, no stop signs, few real rules it seemed. Traffic was almost always thick. Cars, taxi vans, boda bodas (motorcycle taxis), bicyclists, and pedestrians all seemed to play one big game of "chicken" as they wove in and out, jockeying for position.

Typical traffic in Kampala and suburbs

Young men pushed bicycles loaded with eight crates of soda pop, big bags of charcoal, fruit, other goods, or 30-foot long pieces of re-bar or timber with no red flag on the end.

Hauling crates of soda pop

Hauling bananas, charcoal, etc.

There were huge potholes everywhere. Not little dips, but big holes that everyone had to veer to avoid. A narrow two-way road became a one-lane road as everyone was trying to drive around the potholes deep enough to send a boda boda flying or ruin an axle on a car.

I traveled mostly on the back of a boda boda, even though I knew it was dangerous. I would get to my destination in ten minutes, compared to hours stuffed into a hot taxi van with fifteen other people, enduring a spine-jarring ride with no shock absorbers. Sure, I would occasionally brush against the side of vehicles we passed too closely, but it was no big deal. Then something awful happened. My driver tried to pass another boda and my knee smashed against the other motorcycle. I thought my kneecap was being torn off. I screamed for him to stop. I cried in pain as he helped me off the motorcycle and onto the side of the road. Fortunately, I wasn't seriously hurt, but my leg was bruised for weeks from the smashing it took.

Me on boda boda

Family of 6 on one boda boda

Not long after that, I saw a big SUV hit a boda boda. The

motorcycle, its driver, and the rider all went flying through the air. Traffic continued as if nothing happened. Fortunately, both men were able to walk away from the accident.

CHAPTER 23

THE ELDERS

Kabuye and I went to the village of Mpigi on a Sunday. We delivered basic supplies and food to some of the village elders. You don't often see elderly people in Uganda. For one thing, they are a very small part of the population. In the 1980s, many people died of AIDS, malaria, or fighting in wars and never made it past thirty. Even if they made it through the 1980s, malaria still claims many lives to this day.

Those who make it to fifty and beyond often can't walk well. They don't travel far from home, so we went to their homes. Each person received a warm blanket, soap, washtub, sugar, salt, rice, beans, and kerosene. They were so grateful; it was if we'd just brought each person a million dollars.

Sometimes we all sat outside

Sometimes we were invited inside

No matter how little they had, they always offered something in return. One time it was a meal, served on the grass outside. Another time it was a large cabbage from the garden; another it was a hand-woven mat. Such generosity, when they had so little to spare, was beyond humbling. My favorite gift of all though, was when they would sing a hymn to me in Lugandan. Their love shone through their voices.

Reciprocating gifts

Blankets, soap, bins, food supplies, kerosene

I gave one woman a pair of Dollar Store glasses. The look on her face when she put them on and could *see* for the first time in years was priceless! She could finally see well enough to read her Bible or the newspaper again.

These people live with such dignity. Imagine living in a country where you don't have running water in your home. You must walk a half-mile or more to fill your jerry cans with water, then carry the heavy cans back home. Imagine not having the money to buy aspirin or cough medicine, if they were even available. Imagine no option for senior assisted living homes or Medicare or even wheelchairs for mobility. Imagine not being able to see because you've needed glasses for years, or maybe even have cataracts, but no optometrist is in your village. Even if there were a doctor, you wouldn't have the money to pay. Imagine not having a dentist in your village. Imagine having to squat over a hole to go to the bathroom each day, when your joints are so arthritic you can barely move. And imagine all of this while having to raise several toddler grandchildren because their parents died of malaria. You must also do the cooking, tend the garden, and figure out some way to raise a few shillings to buy basic supplies. This is what the "golden years" are like for many Ugandans. After meeting these wonderful elders, my worries about possibly having Alzheimers someday seemed so small.

A family outside a home in Mpigi

CHAPTER 24

THE BARBER

In my free time between comedy shows or visits to the village school, I'd often sit in the barber saloon next to my hotel. I'd chat with Ben the barber and his customers while watching him shave heads. There were many times when the power would suddenly shut off, and he and his customers would be forced to just wait until it came back on again. During those times he helped me learn Lugandan. He'd teach me a phrase, and then I'd try it out on his next customer.

I also wrote jokes that he helped me translate into Lugandan so that when I performed I could do it in the audience's language. He was patient, and instrumental in helping me prepare for each of my comedy shows.

Ben the barber shaving a young girl's head

I had originally suspected that Ben might be gay, but I was wrong. He and I laughed about it. He had a wife, four children, and two toddler nephews to support. They all lived in a small two-room house with no electricity. Ben would arrive at his saloon each morning at 8am, staying until 10pm each night, seven days a week, trying to earn enough money to support his family. He made a tiny amount of money, about $20 dollars on an exceptionally good day, but usually far less. Nearly half went to the shop owner for rent.

He often did not eat because he didn't have enough money for even a cheap lunch. Unlike many of the people I had met here, not once had he asked me for ANYTHING. Many people here saw a white American woman, assumed I was rich and saw me as their only hope. They either immediately asked for help, or they'd wait until the time was right, then asked for money, sponsorship, gifts, an education, or to take them to the USA. Sometimes they would just hint for the help they needed. They would tell me they'd had a dream about me the previous night, in which I had taken them back to America. I didn't blame them. If I were in their place, I might have done the same thing.

But Ben never asked for anything. He showed himself to be an honest, dignified man of integrity who worked hard, day in and day out for his family, with very little hope for the future. He barely made enough for his family to survive; sending his children to school, where everyone must pay tuition, was out of the question.

Two very bad things happened while I was in Ben's acquaintance. First, his electric shaver broke. That was his livelihood. He had to close the shop for half a day and pay for a ride into downtown Kampala to buy a new shaver. The first shaver they tried to sell him was a fake. When he finally got a good one and came back, the shop owner was there waiting. She told him that she was now going to raise his rent AND charge him an electricity fee each month as well. This would mean that he would now not even make enough money to feed his family. He was a defeated, broken man.

I decided to give him his Christmas gift early. It was already wrapped and I was planning to surprise him with it on Christmas Eve. I gave him a box that had a few small gifts in it. His eyes glistened with tears and gratitude -- his parents died of HIV/AIDS when he was a boy, and he had never received a Christmas gift in his life until now.

"Look in the tissue at the bottom of the box, " I said.

He lifted the tissue and immediately burst into huge sobs of relief, joy, and gratitude.

"Sharonee, webale nnyo, nnyo, nnyo," he cried. "Thank you so, so, so much."

Inside the box was a small amount of money. Not enough to change his life. Not enough to buy his own saloon. It was enough to make a difference though.

Here's the kind of man this barber was. He decided to spend that night thinking about how he should spend the money. Many people might spend the money on furniture or clothes or luxury items. The following morning when Ben came to the saloon, he told me that the money would be used to enroll his children in school.

Perhaps THIS was why I was here in Uganda.

CHAPTER 25

CHRISTMAS IN AFRICA

This would be my first Christmas away from my family. I knew we would Skype on Christmas Day if the power was on and the Internet was working. Until then, I kept as busy as possible in the days leading up to Christmas.

I had several comedy shows, including some with a different troupe, the Crackers, meaning people who crack jokes. They performed at Theatre La Bonita. This was a huge, thousand-seat theater with a balcony and velvet seats. Getting to perform here was akin to getting to perform on Broadway in the USA.

Theatre La Bonita

View from the balcony

I prepared new jokes for each of these shows, and memorized them in both Lugandan and Runyankole, since the audience would include people from both tribes.

"Olli otya! Nsanyuse nyo okubalaba!" I would greet the Bagandans.

"Nogambaki! Nashemererwa okukureba!" I would greet the Banyankoles.

On stage at Theatre La Bonita

I would joke in their tribal languages about the boda bodas, the taxi vans, police who stopped people for bribes, the pervasive mud, and whatever else they could relate to. I had gone to get a massage earlier in the week, and was shocked that the woman hit me after she finished with each section of my body! It didn't hurt, but it was definitely an unusual massage technique. So I joked about that too. I brought a man from the audience up on stage and demonstrated.

Demonstrating Ugandan massage

My set aired on Ugandan television the following week. People began to recognize me around Kampala.

Then I was invited to perform with a third troupe. This one was called U-Turn Fun Factory, and they performed outside at Hotel Africana. They did sketch comedy. For this show, I was given a traditional Bagandan gown to wear. It is called a Gomesi.

Wearing a Gomesi for sketch with Fun Factory

I played the part of a Baganda woman who was in a game show. I claimed to be the granddaughter of the Nkima tribe. The audience roared with laughter, at the thought of a Muzungu being from the Nkima tribe.

The week before Christmas, Kabuye and I made another visit to the school. This time I was going to surprise each of the sixty-five students with little bags of candy and toys I had brought in my suitcase. Kabuye had also used some of my money to buy a piece of clothing for each of the children.

We arrived at the school, and just like before, the children were ecstatic, hugging me and screaming with delight. We went inside, and I put on a Santa hat and yelled in a big low voice, "Ho! Ho! Ho!" They might have thought I had just gone a little crazy.

I'm not sure if they knew what I was doing, but they certainly understood the little bag of candy and toys given to them. I was so amazed when not a single one of them snatched the bag away or tore it open. Each child, even the youngest pre-schoolers, knelt and thanked me for the gift, and patiently waited until everyone had theirs and were given the okay to open them.

Each child received a gift bag...

...and a piece of clothing

Then it was time for the clothing to be brought in. I hadn't seen what Kabuye had bought with my money. He had asked a woman he knew to go buy one article of clothing for each child. What I hadn't realized was that she was going to the public market to buy old used clothing sent to Africa from a foreign charity. I was shocked when Kabuye came into the classroom and just dumped the clothing out of a big sack and onto the floor. *What???? No!!! This isn't at all what I had in mind!!!* I had wanted the clothing to be new, clean, and neatly folded. These children deserved better than THIS. I was horrified, but I didn't let it show. It was too late to do anything about the situation now.

Each grade level was called up to the pile of clothing on the floor. The children delightedly picked out a shirt or a dress or a pair of pants, and went back to their seats. Some pieces were soiled or torn. The kids seemed perfectly happy.

Then we went outside and I showed them my next surprise. After seeing the lack of playground equipment on my first visit, I had bought jump ropes, soccer balls, volleyballs, a small basketball and hoop, a toy baseball kit, as well as paint boxes and more reading books and crayons. The children gleefully played games and jumped rope until it was time for me to go.

Mande and other students using one of the new jump ropes

As soon as we got in the car to head home, I turned to Kabuye. "The clothes! Why didn't you get NEW clothes??? I feel terrible for those children!"

"Nantongo," he replied, using the Bagandan name that had been bestowed upon me a month earlier, "most of those children usually never receive any clothing at all. That very well could be the *only* piece of clothing they receive all year. It is new to them, and they are happy for it."

I tried to understand. I came from such a different place and needed to learn to not force my values or expectations onto others. But I had so wanted to give each child a fresh new shirt or dress.

The day before Christmas I went to Ben the barber's home and brought his wife and children several presents wrapped in festive paper. His children were shy and polite. I told his wife what a hardworking husband and beautiful family she had.

On Christmas Day I performed with Fun Factory for a special show in the Uganda National Theatre. I felt honored to be included in the program, but my heart wasn't really in it. I was missing my family terribly and couldn't wait to get back to the hotel to Skype with them.

Seeing my husband and my daughter on Christmas, via the Internet, was the best present I could have asked for. I thanked my daughter for the box of goodies she had sent me. She had included M&Ms! Yum!

Afterward, I felt so alone. It was Christmas, and I wasn't with my family. Not only that, but I hadn't seen Kato or Moses since I first came to Uganda more than a month earlier. I wandered around the quiet hotel where I was often the only guest. I eventually ended up at the saloon with Ben. He was still working, even on Christmas, even with few customers. At the end of his shift, he came back to my hotel with me for a few minutes to watch the fireworks from an upper balcony on the fourth floor. It was a nice way to end Christmas Day in the Pearl of Africa.

CHAPTER 26

FUN GONE WRONG

Several weeks after Christmas, my Brain Wash comedian friends invited me to go with them for a day at the beach. Uganda is a landlocked country, but Lake Victoria has several beaches so I jumped at the chance.

We all piled into Brite's parents' van, and happily turned onto Entebbe Road to head for the beach. Halfway there we stopped and bought some local liquor to lighten the mood even more.

We went to Aero Beach. A plane that once belonged to Idi Amin sits on the property. I changed my clothes under one of the wings.

Plane that belonged to Idi Amin, now at Aero Beach

It was a hot day, and I eagerly ran into the water and joined the scores of Ugandans playing in the gentle waves. The water was cool and the sand felt good under my feet, despite the abundance of snail shells. Most of my friends seemed reluctant to come into the water. I figured they might not know how to swim. The water wasn't too deep for quite a length out, though, and I urged them to join me. Some of them did.

Aero Beach on Lake Victoria

Posing with my comedy buddies

As dusk approached, we loaded back into the van and headed home. Back in the hotel, I decided to Google "Lake Victoria" to find out more about it. What I discovered horrified me and sent chills down my spine. Thousands of dead bodies were dumped into the Kagera River during the Rwanda genocide in the 1990s. Many of the bodies floated down the river and into Lake Victoria on the Uganda side.

Also, raw sewage and industrial waste were still regularly being dumped into the lake from various places along the shore in Uganda, Kenya and Tanzania. As if all this wasn't bad enough, a disease called *schistosomiasis*, also known as *bilharzia*, can be contracted from simply swimming in the water. The disease is acquired by invasion into the human body by parasitic worms that grow in snail shells. WHAT?! My mind raced back to all those snail shells I had been stepping on in the water. The worm enters the body through the skin, lays eggs, and new worms grow inside your bloodstream and internal organs and your brain for years. OH MY GOSH!!!!

I was terrified. *What if I had worms inside me right now?* The website said that this could be treated with a prescription of Praziquantel. *What if the pharmacy here doesn't carry that medicine? What if I can't get a prescription for it?* The pharmacies were all closed for the evening, and I spent the night worrying.

The next morning, I practically ran to the neighborhood pharmacy. The pharmacist immediately knew what I was talking about. Thankfully, not only did she have the pills I needed, but she was able to sell them to me without a prescription. Whew! I practically cried with relief.

I contacted my comedian friends and warned them about the disease. I offered to pay for their prescriptions if they wanted to get them. Without exception, they all laughed it off and told me I was being silly. Silly or not, I was glad I had those pills.

CHAPTER 27
WILD GORILLAS

With just a few weeks left, my time in Uganda was coming to an end. I had one last big adventure to look forward to, a Gorilla Trek. There are only two places in the world where one can find gorillas living in the wild: The Bwindi Forest in far western Uganda, and in Tanzania.

Gorillas are in dire danger of becoming extinct thanks to callous killings by poachers. In an effort to stop this, the Ugandan and Tanzanian governments require special permits for tourists to go on guided hikes through the mountains, hoping for a glimpse of the wild gorillas. The permits to go on these treks are quite expensive. Some of the money is used to bribe poachers and nearby villagers to stop killing the gorillas.

I felt selfish for spending the money on this amazing adventure, when my husband wouldn't be there to experience it with me, but he was dead set against going to Uganda. This was one experience that I felt I'd never have a chance to do again, especially if the gorillas didn't survive. So nine months earlier, after I bought my plane ticket to Uganda, I contacted a reputable tour agent in Kampala and made a seventy-five percent deposit on the Gorilla Trek. The agent was named Baluku. He was the Secretary of the Ugandan Board of Tourism, so I felt I could trust him.

Two days after I arrived in Uganda, Baluku came to my hotel and I gave him the remainder of the money in cash. He promised to personally go with me on the Gorilla Trek, and to provide everything I needed, including rubber boots.

The morning of the Gorilla Trek adventure arrived, and at 7am I raced down the stairs to the lobby to greet Baluku. He had a strange look on his face.

"What's wrong, Baluku?" I asked.

"Uh...Madame Sharonee...um...I'm afraid we cannot go on the Gorilla Trek today."

"Oh? Why?"

"My aunt has died and I must transport the body up north."

"Oh, Baluku, I'm so sorry!" Sadly, untimely and unexpected deaths are all too common in Uganda, thanks to malaria, car accidents, or other travails.

"Yes," Baluku continued, "I'm so sorry about this."

"No, I totally understand," I replied. "Will we be able to reschedule?"

"Oh yes, we'll go in two weeks," he assured me, and went on his way. I went upstairs and back to bed.

Two weeks later, I was again ready at 7am. Only this time, Baluku did not show up. Instead, he had sent one of his contractors, Bosco, to take me on the ten-hour journey across Uganda to the Bwindi Mountains. Bosco arrived two hours late.

"What happened, Bosco? I thought we were supposed to leave at 7am?" I asked.

"Oh?" He seemed surprised. "Baluku called me and said he couldn't take you. I had to drive for two hours already this morning to get here from Jinja. Baluku told me you had a workshop to do this morning and wouldn't be ready until 9am anyway."

This made no sense whatsoever. Workshop? What workshop? What was he talking about? Well, there was no time to waste. We were so late now that we would already be arriving after dark. I got into the van and we began our long drive toward the west.

We passed some of the same towns that Kato, Moses, Cyrus, and I had gone through the previous year on our way to safari. All along the way, there were roadside stands with potatoes or tomatoes stacked in little pyramids.

Pyramid stacks of potatoes

Bosco had made this drive many times, transporting tourists for Baluku and other travel agents. He spoke English well, and we had a wonderful time chatting and laughing all morning. I liked Bosco.

When we pulled into a gas station for lunch, Bosco noticed that one of the tires was nearly flat. Sure enough, there was a nail in the tire, and it needed to be changed. This would take another hour, since a tire had to be found first. I spent the time having lunch at a nearby café.

Lunch of matooke, chicken, beans, potatoes, lentils, rice

Afterward I joked around with a group of boda boda guys. Being able to speak Lugandan really helped me make friends quickly. Being a blond white woman didn't hurt either.

Joking around wit the boda boda guys

The tire was finally changed and we continued on our way. Hours later we stopped for gas again. I needed to use the bathroom. While Bosco filled the tank, I went in search of a place that would have an actual toilet instead of a pit latrine. I thought maybe the hotel next to the gas station would have one. I asked at the front office. They said the only public bathroom they had was in the back. I went to the back, and looked. Darn. Just a hole in the cement. But now I was getting desperate, so...

A few minutes later I made my way back to the gas station. The van was gone! Alarmed, I looked around. There it was, parked near the curb. I walked over to it. Bosco wasn't there. The doors were locked. What was going on? Maybe I had taken so long looking for and using a bathroom that Bosco had thought

I was lost? Maybe he had gone looking for me? I went back to the hotel, looking for Bosco. He wasn't there. I returned to the gas station, fighting off the panic that was building in my gut. I found a gas station attendant and was in the middle of asking him if he had seen my driver, when Bosco came strolling up to me.

"Where were you???!!!" I demanded.

"I was in the bathroom,"

I couldn't argue with that, but it sure had been a long time. "I was scared you had left me!" I exclaimed.

Bosco laughed, shaking his head. "I would never leave you like that, Madame Sharonee," he assured me.

Now it was dark and the roads were getting worse. Every rut, pothole, and rock bounced us like we were on a carnival ride. Not the good kind, but the kind of ride where you just wanted off. My patience began to wear thin.

"How much longer do we have, Bosco?" I asked, gripping my seatbelt with white knuckles as we hit another big pothole.

"Only another hour."

"ANOTHER HOUR?" Okay, this was now officially becoming NO FUN. It had been eleven hours since we left my hotel, and this was getting ridiculous. But what choice was there? Turn back? Hardly.

As we continued, the road got narrower and narrower, until it was just a one-lane dirt road. Rain started falling, softly at first, then harder. Now the road was turning into mud. Around one of the bends, on the edge of a cliff, our van got stuck. Great. This was all we needed. We're in the middle of nowhere, with no streetlights or any lights at all except our headlights, and no one around to help push the van. Would we be spending the night here?

Bosco managed to get the gears to go into four-wheel drive, and maneuvered the van out of the mud. Thirty minutes later, we arrived at the cabins where we were to spend the night. There was no electricity, and I had no flashlight. I made my way around the cabin by the light of the flash on my digital camera. Oh! A toilet! A real toilet! Ahhh, all was right with the world again.

At six in the morning I was awakened by a knock on the door. "Madame Sharonee! Madame Sharonee? Bosco needs to see you down in the dining room."

I got dressed and made my way down the grassy path to the rustic dining room.

"You need to see me?" I asked Bosco, yawning.

He and the cabin hotel manager were standing near a table, with serious looks on their faces. "Madame Sharonee, we need to see your passport."

"My passport? I don't have it." I had been warned not to carry a passport or any large amount of money with me, in case bandits stopped our van and tried to rob us.

The pair exchanged concerned looks. They spoke to each other too quickly in their language for me to decipher what they were saying. "Well, can you try to remember the details from your passport and write them on this piece of paper then?" the manager asked at last.

"Sure, no problem." Something was clearly wrong, but I couldn't figure out what it was. I filled out the paper as best

I could, and Bosco hurried me to the van for the thirty-minute drive to the Gorilla Trek site. The hotel manager came along with us.

"Is everything okay, Bosco?" I asked, as we traveled down the road.

"Yes, everything is fine," he replied. I wasn't sure I believed him.

We soon arrived at the Gorilla Trek site, and I joined five other tourists. Three of the young men were biathletes who competed all over the world. The other two were a young Australian couple on their honeymoon.

"Where are your boots?" the Ugandan guide asked me. I was just wearing lightweight sneakers with webbing.

I looked over at Bosco. He shrugged and shook his head. Baluku had promised to bring rubber boots for me, but apparently Bosco hadn't thought of that or gotten the order from Baluku.

"Well, you can't worry about that now," the guide said. "We've got to get going."

I fell in line behind the guide, the biathletes, and the Australian couple. Two young men from the nearby village came along too, to serve as porters if needed. At the back of the group was another Ugandan guide carrying a rifle. I tried not to think about why he might need a rifle.

Now let me just say that I knew this would not be an easy hike. The website had warned that the gorillas, living in the wild as they were, had to be tracked through the rain forest jungle. We might get lucky and find some gorillas fifteen minutes into the hike, or we might hike for hours and never find any. It was the risk we had to be willing to take. Although I was no biathlete,

I had walked for thirty to sixty minutes every day in hilly areas, both at home in my Portland neighborhood and here in Uganda in my Makindye neighborhood. It might not be easy, but I was confident I could keep up.

I was wrong.

As soon as we started out, torrential rain began pounding down upon us. I put on the thin yellow rain poncho I had brought from home. The ground soon turned to mud. The farther up the mountain we hiked, the denser the jungle became. Our guide used a machete to cut a path for us. There was no neatly trimmed, pre-designed trail. We were truly tracking the gorillas through the jungle, sometimes following elephant footprints. Those footprints soon became deep puddles, and we sank up to our shins in mud. My light webbed sneakers and jeans were no match for the mud. I began to lag behind.

On we went, deeper into the jungle, climbing over logs, swatting at mosquitoes, brushing past thorny foliage with spikes that tore at my clothing and left painful scratches. I began to realize I had bitten off more than I could chew. Each step forward meant one more step to take on the way back. We were only thirty minutes into the trek, but I already knew, without a doubt, that this was more than I could handle. I decided it was best to quit now, while I could probably still find my way back on my own.

"I'm sorry," I said, stopping, "but I'm done. I'm going back."

"No, Madame, you must not stop now! You must keep going," the guide with the rifle said to me.

"No, seriously, I know this is too hard for me. I need to stop and go back," I insisted.

"But Madame, you have paid so much for this. You should not stop now, or it will all be for nothing. Please, keep going," the guide cajoled.

"NO! I really know that I cannot do this!"

"Madame, if it gets too hard, we can help you. The porters can help you. And if you truly can't make it, we can bring in the helicopter to take you out."

"You have a helicopter?" I asked, surprised.

"Yes, you know, I think you Americans call them 'stretchers'," he replied.

Oh hellllll, no! There was no way I was going to be carried out of here on a stretcher!

"Well...does it get any easier?" I asked hopefully.

"Uh...no, it gets harder," he replied, not making eye contact. Then he rushed to reassure me, "But I'm SURE we will find the gorillas soon. Please, Madame, let's keep going. You will be glad you did."

Against my better judgment, and probably because this discussion had given me time to catch my breath, I reluctantly agreed to continue. By now the others were far ahead. They stopped and waited for me. I was so embarrassed. I looked exactly like what I was, a fifty-seven year old chubby lady who couldn't keep up and was going to hold everybody back. I urged them to go ahead and not wait for me again. A porter and the guide with the rifle stayed by my side and helped me along.

The terrain got worse and the mountainside grew steeper. Each step required digging a foothold in the mud, and grasping onto vines to pull myself up. I tried to give myself a pep talk. *Come* on, Sharon, you can do this. Attitude is everything. You just have to have the right attitude. Pretend you're in The Amazing Race. The pep talk wasn't working. Sharon, you can do this! Pretend you're on Survivor. Pretend you're a contestant on The Biggest Loser." This wasn't a reality show though, and MY reality right now was that this was grueling.

I tried to stop a moment to rest.

"We must keep going, Madame...the fire ants will bite us." Sure enough, before the guide even finished his sentence, fire ants started biting my ankles and back under my torn poncho. Now I was relying on the porter to help me. He held my arm and guided and pulled me along, catching me if I slipped. I felt so humiliated. Tears began streaming down my face. I was angry, embarrassed, wet, and exhausted.

Up and down the sides of that jungle mountain we trudged. About seven hours – SEVEN HOURS – after we started, the rain stopped and we all gathered in the forest. The others looked a bit tired, but exhilarated and happy. By now, I was just so upset that I honestly was thinking that maybe this was just a ruse to lead foreigners deep into the jungle and kidnap them for ransom.

That was when we found them, a family of wild mountain gorillas. We silently stood there, fifteen feet away from them, gazing in awe of their power, beauty, and innocence.

The largest was a silverback. He was the thirty-five year old patriarch, majestically gnawing on leaves while keeping a watchful eye on us. He had black fur, with silver on the back of his head and shoulders. He was magnificent.

The silverback

Across from him, lying on a mound of vines was a pregnant female. She seemed to be having a hard time finding a comfortable position.

The pregnant female...

...hard to find a comfortable position

Behind her, a young male looked at us and pounded his chest impressively. Two juveniles frolicked in the bushes near him, chasing each other and doing somersaults.

We were allowed to stand silently and take pictures for twenty minutes. The guide offered to take my photo. I declined, partly because I knew I looked like a drenched rat, and also because I didn't feel like I deserved a photo of myself here after the way I had behaved. He insisted, though. So, much as this is still embarrassing to me, here is the photo:

Which one is the gorilla?

We then headed back down the mountain. It was a much faster trip back, since we were angling straight down to the starting point. It took us about an hour. Although it was faster, it was, in some ways, just as difficult as going up. One slip could result in a slide down the mountainside much like Kathleen

Turner in that 1984 movie *Romancing the Stone.* I hung onto the porter tightly most of the way. I apologized that I had no money with me to tip him, since I hadn't been instructed to bring any money. Sincerely, I promised to send him $100 when I got back to Kampala. I figured that the amount would be a fortune to him, and worth the wait. If he understood what I was saying, he didn't show it. He was probably disgusted that I had nothing to give him today, and might have doubted I'd really ever send him anything after all of his hard work today.

As soon as we made it back to the starting site, I ran to Bosco.

"Bosco! I need to borrow some money to tip the guide and the porter," I hurriedly said. "I'll pay you back as soon as we get back to Kampala tomorrow."

"Uh...Madame Sharonee...I am sorry, but I have no money," he said slowly. "And we have no way to get back to Kampala."

I thought I must have misheard him. "I'm sorry, what?"

"We have no way to get back to Kampala," he said, looking miserable.

"What do you mean? What's going on?" I asked, alarmed.

"My van has been confiscated."

"What are you talking about? Why would anyone take your van?" I couldn't believe what I was hearing. But if I thought that was unbelievable, the words that came next were simply absurd.

"You did not pay the Gorilla Trek fees, so unless you can pay now, they are taking my van as collateral," Bosco said, clearly distressed.

"WHAT??? I DID PAY MY FEES!! I sent seventy-five percent of the money to Baluku nine months ago, and I paid him the remainder in full in cash two days after I arrived in Uganda!!" I insisted.

The Park Ranger now joined in. "I'm sorry, Madame, but there is no proof of that. And if this is not paid, we will have to send you to jail. I should not have even allowed you to go on the Trek at all without that permit. The hotel manager and Bosco begged me to let you go, because they were sure there had been some mistake."

"Well, there most certainly HAS been a mistake! I assure you, I have paid everything in full!"

Bosco stepped to my side. "I have been trying to get in touch with Baluku all day to get this all straightened out. In fact, yesterday, at the gas station when you were looking for me, I had been trying to call Baluku. He has not paid me for the gas and other travel expenses for this trip. And he has also not paid the hotel manager for our stay. When I finally got in touch with him from the gas station, he told me that you had paid the money too late, but that he would get it from the bank soon."

"No! That's a lie! I sent him three-fourths of the money NINE MONTHS AGO! And I gave him the rest when I arrived in Uganda!"

"Do you have your receipt?" the park ranger asked.

"No, I didn't think I would need it! In fact, Baluku didn't even give me a receipt for the final amount. But I paid him!" I desperately tried to think of how I could prove that I had paid for this trip. "Do you have a computer and Internet access? If so, I can at least show you proof of payment for most of the trip."

"We can go to my office and try to get a connection," the ranger said. "If you can show me proof of payment, that will keep you out of jail. However, I will still need to keep the van until I actually receive the money."

This was serious. I could end up in a Ugandan jail seven hours away from anyone who could possibly help me. I had no money and no passport. Without those, I couldn't even call anyone to ask them to wire me money.

In his office, the ranger turned on his computer. At first there was no Internet connection. One of his aides fiddled with the equipment, and thankfully the connection came on. I tried to sign in to my Yahoo account so I could show the ranger the email from Baluku, stating he had received my first payment. I typed in my account name and password. I was denied access since this was not my computer! Unbelievable! Could this get any worse?

I don't remember how, but somehow I found a way to get around this block to show the ranger the proof that he needed. What a relief. The ranger believed me.

Baluku had been lying all along. He lied to me about his aunt having died, lied to Bosco about my having to be late because of some bogus workshop, lied again to Bosco, claiming I had made a late payment. And he lied a final time, saying he'd get back in touch soon. Baluku was nowhere to be found. Clearly, whatever he had done with my money, it hadn't been to pay the bills and permit fees that were owed.

I was in the clear. We still had the problem of how to get back to Kampala, since Bosco's van would remain impounded until my permit fee was paid. The ranger gave us a ride back to the cabins. We hoped Bosco would be able get a cell phone signal there so he could call relatives in Kampala for money to be wired to him.

It took a long time, but Bosco was finally able to reach his relatives. Unfortunately, none of them had that amount of money on hand, and it would be days before they could gather enough to send to him. We were at a dead end.

It was late, and all we could do for now was spend the night in the hotel cabins and try to figure out something in the morning. I was so grateful to the manager for allowing us to stay another night, since she had yet to be paid anything for the rooms or the food provided to us.

The next morning, the only thing I could think to do was to hitchhike back to Kampala on my own. I would get the money I had in my hotel room and wire it to Bosco so he could get his van back. Was this a foolish idea? Absolutely, but Bosco had put everything on the line for me. He could have just as easily have said, "No, I don't vouch for her, and I'm not willing to put my van up for collateral. Throw her in jail. Buh-bye." He hadn't. He had shown tremendous valor and courage, and I needed to do everything I could to help him in return.

I had just enough small change in my pocket to pay for a boda boda ride to the nearest village. From there I figured I could make a sign, "KAMPALA", and try to get a ride across the country.

Just as I was getting onto the boda boda, Bosco came racing toward me.

"Wait! Wait!" he called to me. "Don't go! I got a loan!!!"

A loan company in Kampala had agreed to wire him the money he needed, at an outrageous 300% interest. Disgusting. But what else were we to do? He accepted the terms, the money was wired, and he paid the ranger and was given back his keys. We were on our way home within the hour.

One might think that this was the end of the story. It wasn't.

On the way home we had not one, but TWO more flat tires. And the spare tire was flat, too. Seriously? This was so beyond unbelievable it was starting to be funny. The first flat happened as we drove through Mbarara, so that was a fairly quick fix. The second one happened about two miles past Mbarara, on the dark highway.

We couldn't drive the van back to Mbarara with a flat tire, so the only choice we had was for Bosco to roll the tire back to the town while I stayed with the van. By the side of the road, late at night, submerged in darkness except for the headlights of passing cars.

In comparison to everything else I had already been through, this seemed like nothing. I stayed in the van for a while, but then I saw three very small children approaching the van.

I got out to greet them. They looked like they were about three to five years old. What were they doing wandering alone at this time of night? They didn't know English. I tried speaking to them in Lugandan. Blank stares. Then I tried Runyankole. AHA!! CONNECTION!

They smiled and giggled as I asked them their names and told them my name. Now what? They were little ones, so I decided to count to ten on my fingers in their language. They counted with me. This game was fun! Then I named animals in their language, and they made the sound the animal would make. Now the children were giggling and laughing even more.

They trusted me so much by now, that one of them decided she wanted to touch my white arm. I let her. She let out a squeal of delight. Then she pointed to my leg. I think she wondered if my leg was white, too. So I pulled up the hem of my jeans to show her my white leg. "Ohhhhh!!!" Screams of laughter. They all wanted to touch my leg and arms.

An idea struck me. I figured if these kids had never seen or touched a Muzungu before, then maybe they had never had their picture taken either. I got my digital camera out of the van and took their picture. The flash blinded them temporarily in the extreme darkness. When I showed them their picture on the screen, their excitement was through the roof! They begged me to take their picture again and again, so I did.

Children who kept me company in the dark

Right about then, their older brother came looking for them. I smiled at him and greeted him, and he smiled back. He told them they had to go home and go to bed. They didn't want to leave me, and the boy was too curious to leave too. So in a short while, the father came looking for all of them and sent them running down the side of the hill to their home.

Bosco arrived soon after that, fixed the tire, and we were on our way. That interaction with the children had erased all of the stress of the past two days. We made it back to Kampala, and I gave Bosco enough money to cover the loan he had gotten for the van. It was the least I could do, after all he had done for me.

The next day Bosco and I went to the Kampala police station and filed a police report against Baluku. Then we went to the Ugandan Board of Tourism to report what had happened. These were very serious charges against their board secretary, and they had a hard time believing us.

"Surely this must all just be a misunderstanding. Baluku will surely have a reasonable explanation," was the response we got. They tried to reach him on the phone. No answer. They sent someone to his home to get him. No one was there. Baluku was in hiding.

At last the Board agreed that this was a serious situation, and they called a meeting of all the travel agents across Uganda to be held the following afternoon.

Before the meeting began, someone was able to get Baluku on the phone, and told him to come to this meeting. He said he would. We waited for nearly four hours. Someone finally went and picked him up and brought him to the meeting.

His head was hanging low as he came into the boardroom avoiding eye contact. The Board Chairman asked Baluku if he had an explanation for what had happened. Baluku mumbled that his girlfriend had taken the money from him. Then he mumbled a quick, meager apology.

The Board Chairman asked me if I would accept the apology and drop the charges. I couldn't believe my ears! Drop the charges after all he had put Bosco and me through, hidden from us, and then gave a wimp of an apology??? I should have known this would happen. It had been quietly confided to me in private before the meeting that the Board Chairman and Baluku were from the same tribe. In fact, the Chairman had even suggested taking up a donation to help the poor guy out of this mess!

"I have something to say," I answered. "Baluku, I want you to know what you put us through. You tried to disparage my character. You called me a liar. You tried to put the blame of your crime onto me. I could be sitting in jail right now because of you, if it were not thanks to the brave man sitting across the table from you."

I pointed to Bosco.

"Baluku, I want you to look at Bosco. He was your FRIEND. And what did you do? You left him high and dry with no money, just more lies. This man could have just left me at Bwindi and driven back home. But he didn't. He refused to leave me. He stayed there until he was able to get a loan at 300% to get his van back so he could take me safely back home. All because of the position you put us in. Baluku, this man, BOSCO, has MORE COURAGE in his little finger than you will ever have. More than me, you owe HIM an apology. A SINCERE apology."

Baluku apologized to Bosco, with more sincerity than before.

"And one more thing, Baluku," I continued. "If I ever hear that there are any repercussions against Bosco, or if he loses any work because of this, I will hold YOU personally responsible. DO you understand me?"

Baluku nodded.

Then I addressed the Chairman. "Now. What about the hotel manager and the park ranger? How will they be paid? And how will Bosco be reimbursed for his expenses?"

The Chairman promised that he personally would pay for all of these debts, and that Baluku would be held accountable and reprimanded.

The meeting was adjourned.

A few days later, I checked to be sure that the bills had been paid. They had been. As promised, I also wired $100 to the porter.

CHAPTER 28

SAYING GOODBYE

It was time to head back to Oregon. Kato and Moses came to visit a few days before I had to leave and it was wonderful to see them again.

Ben had quit his job at the saloon. He just saw no reason to work all day, only to hand his money over to the owner. I agreed with his decision. In fact, it finally occurred to me that I was probably the reason all this happened in the first place. An American becomes friends with the barber? Surely that must mean she is giving him money, right? So why not take a cut of that money and raise the rent?

I told Ben my suspicions, and he couldn't deny the probability. I felt terrible. Our friendship was hurting him, this man who had done nothing wrong but be my friend. The only thing I could think to do to help make things right was to buy him a small generator so he could shave heads out of his home.

One day, as I was walking past the café/saloon, the owner came out and greeted me. She acted very friendly, as if we were buddies. She inquired if it might be possible to get a small loan from me. I looked at her with disgust.

"You must be joking," I said. "After what you did to Ben, you are the last person I would loan money to." Her jaw dropped as I breezily brushed past her and continued on down the road.

Ben and his best friends, Michael and William, escorted me to the airport. We all cried as I hugged each one goodbye. I would miss them. I would miss all of Uganda. It had truly been an adventure.

Ben, William, and Michael at the airport

CHAPTER 29

A FUNNY THING HAPPENED...

It's been four years since that trip to Uganda. Since then, I've headlined in many more clubs and casinos, including in Hawaii, Alaska, and New York City. These days I do lots of corporate comedy entertainment and give motivational speeches. I have found my "voice" and my comedy material leans far toward the clean side rather than raunchy.

I've been back to Uganda two more times, performing comedy and bringing aid to the children and the elderly, including a second school in Nkumba. This school had two hundred students, but no latrine. They now have a six-hole latrine, desks, and more, thanks to the money I've raised by selling homemade bracelets after my comedy shows in the USA. I'm also helping put Mande through college, and am paying all school fees for Ben's children.

My mom died on November 1, 2015 at the age of eighty-three. She didn't know who I was, but I was sitting by her side and holding her hand as she took her last breath, just as I was with Grama.

Now my dad is in the early stages of Alzheimer's.

A funny thing happened on my way to dementia; I didn't get there. Not yet, anyway. I'm only sixty-one, so who knows what will happen in the coming years. But in these last eleven years,

I've learned that we can take our challenges and turn them into opportunities to learn, to grow, to make connections, and to help other people.

I wouldn't change a thing.

The proceeds from this book will go to help the people of Uganda, Africa.

Video clips from Sharon's trips to Uganda are available on YouTube.

If you'd like to book Sharon for a speaking engagement, go to:
www.sharonlaceycomedy.com

CPSIA information can be obtained
at www.ICGtesting.com
Printed in the USA
LVOW10s1743100317
526811LV00010B/873/P